THE
INTERNATIONAL
MONETARY
MECHANISM

LELAND B. YEAGER
University of Virginia

HOLT, RINEHART AND WINSTON, INC.
New York · Chicago · San Francisco · Atlanta
Dallas · Montreal · Toronto · London

FOREWORD

In recent years the fiscal and monetary tools economists have fashioned to achieve national economic goals have undergone considerable refinement. They are, however, still crude and awkward devices and our understanding of monetary influences remains very limited. Nevertheless, the responsibility placed upon the United States monetary policy for achieving national economic objectives has been accelerating. There is every need therefore for this process of development, refinement and sharpening to continue, that is, ideas must be developed, their implications tested and the theory then revised and retested.

The Holt, Rinehart and Winston series in Money and Banking includes the following titles: *The International Monetary Mechanism, Monetary Policy, Supply and Demand for Money, Banking History: The U. S. Experience, The Money Market,* and *Financial Institutions.* The series is designed to serve a number of objectives. First, the complete collection of titles provides the instructor with a self-contained text in *Money and Banking*; second, quality monographs are provided to supplement standard textbooks in both elementary and advanced courses in money and banking and in related courses; third, the series provides the student with those tools and techniques of monetary analysis which will enable him to better understand the role of monetary influences upon the economy and the functioning of the international monetary mechanism.

By combining both comprehensiveness and depth of analysis, the series provides the instructor with a number of options. Each monograph is authored by an outstanding scholar; hence, the instructor is provided with the opportunity to employ the writings of specialized experts either for selected topics or throughout the entire course, enabling the student to obtain the benefit of each author's expertise.

Each volume is a rigorous, analytical, virtually self-contained effort which stresses systematic forms of analysis. Alternative theories are explained, their empirical content is noted, and the available evidence compared with their predictions. Exercises for student drill are provided whenever possible to test the student's mastery of the concepts and tools of analysis that are developed in each chapter. Thus, the terminal student in money and banking obtains a firmer understanding of the role of money and financial assets in the economy, while the student who plans to continue his studies in this field is provided with a markedly stronger foundation in monetary analysis.

William Beranek, *Adviser*
MONEY AND BANKING SERIES

PREFACE

When Professor William Beranek asked me to write this little book, Harper & Row, publishers of my *International Monetary Relations,* encouraged me to go ahead. They realized that although the two books would overlap, they would aim at different markets. Harper & Row have my sincere thanks. Readers who want fuller treatment of topics or justification of conclusions than this book offers will perhaps find them in the larger work. This book is new, however, in arrangement, in most of the wording, and in much of the content. For permission to draw on several pages of *Trade Policy and the Price System,* I am also indebted to my co-author, Professor David Tuerck, and to our publisher, International Textbook Company.

Without implicating him in any mistakes of mine, I want to thank Professor Alexandre Kafka, Executive Director of the International Monetary Fund, for illuminating discussions about some important operational details of the existing international monetary system and of modifications likely to be adopted.

Since my text had already been set in type, it was not practical— nor was it necessary—to revise it after intergovernmental efforts to hold down the price of gold on the London market collapsed in March 1968. The gold pool then gave way to a two-price system. My pages on gold even gain in significance because they help explain what attitudes and actions of private speculators forced that change in policy. Whether the change will turn out to have weakened those speculative attitudes only slightly or to have eliminated them almost completely will depend on whether the continued pegging of the official gold price at $35 allows only partial uncertainty or allows completely unbiased two-way uncertainty about which way the free-market price will move. For central bankers, the apparent one-way-only changeability of the official gold price remains as relevant as before. Another problem will be that of keeping the official and free gold markets separated. For these and other reasons, the two-price system may prove only a temporary expedient intended to buy time for solving the American balance-of-payments problem, for activating the "special drawing rights" described in Chapter 8, and perhaps for making more fundamental reforms in the international monetary system. The chapters on alternative systems have therefore become even more topical now than when they were written.

To avoid footnotes, I have put at the end of each chapter a list of writings either suggested for further reading or alluded to in the text. These references appear in roughly the same order as the related topics in the chapter.

Charlottesville, Virginia   Leland B. Yeager
April 1968

CONTENTS

1

THE "REAL" SIDE OF

INTERNATIONAL ECONOMICS

The international monetary mechanism, like national monetary systems, exists to promote efficiency in making and exchanging goods and services. Money and prices convey information about real economic opportunities and guide responses to them. This chapter briefly reviews what even a first course in economics should stress about the realities that underlie money and prices.

THE GAIN FROM TRADE

Ideally, under competition, prices indicate opportunity costs—how much each good costs in forgone production of other things. Suppose we can produce widgets in our country for $5 each. This means, under ideal competitive conditions, that producing a widget costs forgoing production of other goods that would also have been worth $5 to us. Suppose, now, that we can buy widgets abroad for only $3. If imports and exports pay for each other (a tendency examined later), an imported widget costs us $3 worth of our export products. To supply these exports we must sacrifice consuming them or sacrifice producing and consuming other goods that would also have been worth $3 to us. Importing a widget at $3 thus costs us only three-fifths as much sacrifice of other things as would making it ourselves at $5. In effect we "produce" widgets indirectly, and more efficiently than by producing them directly, by producing other things to trade away for them. Importing a product at a money price below the cost of making it ourselves yields a real saving of other things forgone.

> Individual persons and companies (and some government agencies) carry on trade, of course, not "countries" as such. Similarly, only *people* gain or lose from economic developments or policies; the concept of gain or loss for a country as a whole is fuzzy. This fuzziness besets economic theory and policy in general, however, and not international monetary economics in particular. Here we permit ourselves the convenience of saying that "our country" carries on trade and reaps the gain. The gain is of the same admittedly debatable kind as gain from inventions or from miraculous abolition of hurricanes, since almost any change harms *somebody*. We should remember that we are using convenient metaphors. We should beware of personifying countries to the extent of not really knowing what we mean about the actions and experiences of individual persons, companies, and official agencies. The importance of this warning will become clearer in Chapter VII.

Our opportunity for gain from cheap imports is genuine regardless of *why* foreigners sell so cheaply, regardless of any "distortions" inside their economies. What matters to us is whether prices in our own country correctly indicate how much each product costs in required sacrifice of others. Many people fail to understand this. They warn that trade is falsely based and harmful unless goods of the kinds imported are produced with greater *absolute* or *physical* efficiency abroad than in the importing country. A reply to this error need not rest on quibbling about how elusive the notion of absolute efficiency is. We can assume an extreme case for the sake of argument: producing a unit of each product requires larger physical amounts of labor and every other factor of production abroad than at home. Yet trade can be beneficial if the foreigners, with their all-across-the-board inferior efficiency, specialize in the lines of production where their inferiority is the slightest, while we, with our all-across-the-board superior efficiency, specialize in the lines of our greatest superiority. International comparisons of factor requirements or absolute efficiency are a red herring; what counts is comparing the opportunities available in domestic production and in foreign trade.

COMPARATIVE ADVANTAGE

This *principle of comparative advantage* is an "even if" proposition: it demonstrates how trade can yield benefits *even* in a farfetched case that might seem to rule trade out. Actually, the principle is unnecessary for explaining the gains from trade; elaborating on the example of the $5 and the $3 widgets would serve nicely. But to convince people who insist on comparing absolute efficiencies, the principle accepts their premises for the sake of argument. The example of Jones and Smith marooned on a desert island will remind the reader of what he probably understands already. In an hour of work, Jones could pick 9 coconuts *or* catch 3 fish, while Smith could pick 4 coconuts *or* catch 2 fish. Jones is superior in producing both goods. He is more superior in coconut-picking, though, since in an hour he can pick 125 percent more coconuts than Smith but can catch only 50 percent more fish. Smith has a *comparative advantage* in fishing, his less inferior work. Both men gain if each specializes in his own comparatively advantageous work and if they trade coconuts for fish on terms somewhere between Jones's 3:1 ratio and Smith's 2:1 ratio of coconut-production capacity to fish-production capacity. As the example stresses, the principle of comparative advantage does not call for having each task done by the man who can do it most efficiently. That would mean having Jones divide his time between fishing and coconut-picking, while Smith does nothing. The gain comes, instead, from each man's concentrating on the work in which he is more superior or less inferior.

The same point carries over to international trade. The principle of comparative advantage does *not* recommend always making each product wherever it could be made at lowest cost in inputs used. Instead, the principle shows the gain from letting each country specialize in whatever goods it can make at lowest cost in other production forgone. Under competition, money costs and prices indicate cheapness in this fundamental opportunity-cost sense.

PRICES AND EXCHANGE RATES

Practical businessmen and consumers neither know nor need to know anything about comparative advantage and opportunity cost. They want to buy where *money prices* are lowest and sell where *money prices* are highest. But if all lines of production really were less efficient abroad than in our country, how could foreigners price any of their goods low enough to sell them in our market? How could foreigners pay for any purchases from us? The answer hinges on a generally low level of wages and other incomes abroad ("low" as translated at appropriate exchange rates and compared with our wage and income levels). Low wage levels—the famous "cheap foreign labor"—are an inevitable result of the foreigners' relatively low over-all efficiency or productivity, but they are also what enables foreigners to sell us the goods in which their disadvantage is smallest and to pay for our goods that they could make themselves only at relatively great disadvantage. Low wages let the foreigners take part in beneficial international trade and so become less poor than otherwise. We also gain, even when trading with inefficient, ill-paid foreigners. Shrinkage of particular industries in our country does not prove otherwise. Shifting labor and resources out of our least superior into our most superior lines of production is a key part of the process of reaping the gains from trade.

Under competition, a pattern of prices and exchange rates emerges at which consumers and profit-seeking businessmen have the incentives to conduct the trade yielding the gain described by the principles of comparative advantage and opportunity cost. No one has to measure directly how much each product costs in forgone physical output of others. No one has to take these opportunity costs consciously into account. As long as the economic system corresponds fairly well to the competitive model, money costs and prices measure these opportunity costs; and people have ordinary profit-and-loss incentives to heed them. Suppose that opportunity costs at home and abroad are reflected in prices of $6 a yard for cloth and $2 a bushel for wheat in our country and prices of 36 pesos for cloth and 18 pesos for wheat abroad. To know where they can buy each good cheap or sell it dear, businessmen must consider the exchange rate. At more than 9 pesos per dollar, both goods would be cheaper abroad. The foreigners would export both and import neither. This imbalance could not last if cloth and wheat were the only tradable goods (and if international transactions comprised commodity trade only, as we also assume for simplicity). At the opposite extreme, a rate of fewer than 6 pesos per dollar would make both goods cheaper in our country. A workable exchange rate must fall somewhere between 9 and 6 pesos per dollar, the exact rate being the one at which each country's exports and imports are equal in total money value.

A more elaborate example, involving several products rather than only two, would further emphasize how different patterns of relative prices within countries, reflecting different patterns of opportunity costs, set the stage for determining what goods each country will export and import. (Relative prices are price ratios. In the example just given, the relative prices are three bushels of wheat for one yard of cloth in our country and two for one abroad.) Exchange rates translate differences in opportunity costs and relative prices into differences in absolute prices. The cheaper one country's currency is in relation to other curencies, the wider will be the range of that country's products underselling similar foreign products and the greater will be the amount of its currency that foreigners demand per time period to buy its relatively cheap goods. (This is one of the reasons why the law of demand holds true for currencies in the foreign-exchange market as well as for ordinary commodities in ordinary markets.) A workable exchange rate between each two currencies would enable each country's total exports just to pay for its total imports (we are still assuming away such complications as international lending). What goods each country exports and imports and what pattern of exchange rates would make trade balance depend on how strong the preferences for the various goods are, on how much local prices (reflecting opportunity costs) would change in each country as the pattern of production responded to trade, and on the height of each country's average price level in its own currency.

Trade does not leave prices in local currency unchanged in the trading countries. The addition of foreign to local supplies lowers the local prices of import-type goods; the addition of foreign to local demands raises the prices of export goods. Were it not for transportation costs, tariffs, and other obstacles to trade, as well as imperfections in competition, the prices of each good would move toward being everywhere the same, as translated at the exchange rates emerging from the same process. This international equalization of prices of goods (and opportunity costs at the margin) would not destroy trade. It would destroy only the incentives for its further expansion (except, of course, as underlying conditions such as population, tastes, and technology changed). In a sense, though, the trade would still be motivated by *virtual* or *latent* price differences, differences that would have persisted in its absence and that would appear if trade were cut off or restricted.

These (virtual) differences in absolute prices as made comparable by exchange rates rest on different patterns of relative prices and opportunity costs in the different countries. What underlies and explains these different price patterns? In each country some factors of production are more abundant and cheaper in comparison with other factors than in the outside world; other factors are relatively scarce and expensive. In the absence of trade, goods whose production uses relatively large amounts of a country's abundant factors tend to be relatively cheap; goods requiring large amounts of scarce factors are expensive. This, however, is only part of the story. In fact, (virtual) differences in patterns of relative prices stem from unfathomably complex differences among countries in resources, populations, tastes, ideologies, and natural, social, and political climates. Whatever the reasons may be, countries do have comparative advantages in different lines of production; hence, trade can offer gains akin to the gains from technological progress. Profit incentives lead businessmen to engage in trade yielding the gains the theory describes. Exchange rates emerge at which trade tends to balance. Each country can then undersell foreigners in some products and export them—the products in which it has a comparative advantage. At the same time, foreigners can undersell the country in its home market in import products in which it has a comparative disadvantage.

This whole process is simplest to explain if exchange rates are flexible. If they are fixed, the different patterns of relative prices within countries have to become transformed into appropriate absolute price differences between countries in a way more complicated to explain. National money supplies and average price levels have to adjust so as to keep the fixed exchange rates appropriate. Chapter 5 describes this process and also looks more closely at how flexible exchange rates work.

REFERENCES

1. GOTTFRIED HABERLER. *A Survey of International Trade Theory*. Revised and Enlarged Edition. International Finance Section, Princeton University, 1961.

2. W. M. CORDEN. *Recent Developments in the Theory of International Trade*. International Finance Section, Princeton University, 1965.

3. LELAND B. YEAGER and DAVID G. TUERCK. *Trade Policy and the Price System*. Scranton, Pa.: International Textbook Company, 1966.

INTERNATIONAL PAYMENTS
AND FOREIGN EXCHANGE

INTERNATIONAL PAYMENTS

The goods and services moving in private international trade are priced and paid for in ordinary national currencies. Loans and investments are also expressed in national money. Private business firms and banks use no special kind of international money. What "international liquidity" might mean, then, and what problems involve it are questions postponed until Chapter 7.

An American importer buying British goods priced in pounds sterling pays in sterling funds on deposit in a British bank. He transfers the money to his British supplier by a draft, check, or cabled order that he buys for dollars from his own bank in the United

States. His bank, or a larger American bank with which his bank has a correspondent relationship, has been holding a sterling deposit in a British bank for just such purposes. The American bank is continually replenishing its sterling deposit by buying checks and similar claims on British bank balances from American exporters and other customers who have been receiving payments in sterling.

If the British exporter in this example has priced his goods and has received payment in dollars rather than sterling, it is he, rather than his American customer, who takes the initiative in exchanging dollars for sterling. The difference is unimportant. When the Briton receives payment in a dollar check, he sells it for sterling to his own bank, which has the amount credited to its dollar deposit in an American bank. The British bank maintains such a deposit as an inventory from which to sell dollars to British importers and other customers needing dollars.

THE FOREIGN-EXCHANGE MARKET

Only by great coincidence would a bank's sales and purchases of foreign money in transactions with its own customers exactly match each other. In each country, some banks are developing a shortage and others a surplus of foreign money. The banks can largely even out their positions by buying and selling foreign bank balances among each other. Every major financial center has an interbank or "wholesale" market in foreign exchange. (Although it includes actual foreign coins and banknotes, foreign exchange consists mostly of claims on foreign currency, such as bank accounts and short-term negotiable paper.) The banks deal with each other by telephone—usually, for convenience, through the intermediary of brokers.

It would still be a coincidence if the banks in each country were buying no more and no less of each foreign money from their customers than they were selling to their customers. Perhaps American banks are acquiring too many pounds sterling, while British banks are acquiring too many dollars. Then the solution is obvious. International telephone and teleprinter facilities link the individual financial centers together into a single worldwide foreign-exchange market (except as government controls hamper this unification). Because of this linkage, it does not much matter whether the British goods imported into the United States are priced and paid for in dollars or in sterling. In either case, dollars appear on the market in exchange for sterling. The difference concerns merely whether the British exporter takes the initiative on the British retail sector of the worldwide foreign-exchange market or the American importer takes the initiative on the American sector.

Imbalances in some geographic sectors of the world foreign-exchange market can cancel out opposite imbalances in others. But what, if anything, assures the *overall* balance that permits the mutual offsetting of local imbalances? Under a system of freely flexible rates, the foreign-exchange market clears itself in much the same way as a competitive market for any ordinary commodity does: each exchange rate, like an ordinary price, moves to the level at which supply and demand are equal. When a system of fixed exchange rates prevents this automatic clearing, central banks or other government agencies buy and sell on the market to absorb surpluses and supply deficiencies of foreign currencies at the fixed rates. How extensively and how long the government agencies can keep on doing so, and with what consequences, are questions to be discussed later.

EQUILIBRIUM ON THE FOREIGN-EXCHANGE MARKET

For a simple explanation of what keeps the foreign-exchange market cleared, let us consider American transactions with the rest of the world as a whole. We shall lump all foreign currencies together under the name "foreign exchange." This simplification is legitimate; for in the absence of restrictions, one foreign currency can be sold for any other almost instantly at a competitively determined exchange rate belonging to a consistent pattern of rates. *Multilateral currency arbitrage* maintains this consistency. (Arbitrage consists of dealing to profit from discrepancies between prices prevailing at the same time in different submarkets.) Suppose, for example, that the "broken cross rates" prevailed of 60 Belgian francs per dollar, 10 Belgian francs per German mark, and 3 German marks per dollar. An arbitrageur (typically a large bank) could profit by buying 60 francs with $1, buying 6 marks with the 60 francs, and buying $2 with the 6 marks. Transactions like this on a large scale would strengthen the franc against the dollar (perhaps toward a rate of 50 francs per dollar), strengthen the mark against the franc (perhaps toward 12½ francs per mark), and strengthen the dollar against the mark (perhaps toward 4 marks per dollar). This or some such consistent pattern of rates would emerge at which no further arbitrage was profitable. Even small discrepancies of the sort exaggerated here would motivate enough arbitrage to wipe them out in a few minutes.

Let us suppose that some disturbance to overall balance in transactions makes American purchases of goods, services, and claims abroad exceed American sales abroad. Desired purchases of foreign exchange with dollars exceed desired sales of foreign exchange for dollars. On a market free from official manipulation, this imbalance would bid up the price of foreign exchange in dollars (reduce the value of dollars in foreign money). As translated at the new exchange rate, the higher dollar prices of foreign goods, services, and claims would cause Americans to buy fewer of them. At the same time, foreigners would buy more American goods, services, and claims because they had become cheaper in foreign money. The totals of desired transactions in the two directions would become equal again (no doubt at a changed level) because the exchange rate would move to just the necessary figure. If the adjustment should overshoot the mark and make the dollar too weak on the foreign-exchange market, the rate would move back toward its new equilibrium level, just as the dollar would strengthen toward a new equilibrium if the initial disturbance had been the opposite of the kind we assumed. (Chapter 5 considers this balancing process in more detail.)

OFFICIAL EXCHANGE STABILIZATION

In the real world of constant change in national price levels, tastes, technology, weather, political conditions, and other factors, flexible exchange rates would be responding with continual (though usually mild) fluctuations. For various reasons (reviewed in later chapters), governments usually hold exchange rates almost rigid, apart from rare deliberate adjustments. When a country's currency shows signs of weakening under the pressure of excess imports of goods, services, and securities, the central bank or other official agency supports it by buying it with foreign exchange (or gold) held in reserve for that purpose. In doing so, the agency fills the gap between the total value of imports of goods, services, and securities and the smaller value of exports. Actually, the agency maintains as well as fills the gap; for if it were not filled, it could not exist. Instead, the value of the country's imports (in the broad sense considered here) would necessarily shrink to the value of its exports in some way or other—by depreciation of the home currency or by controls designed to choke off demands for foreign exchange. The agency can go on filling the gap only as long as it has reserves left or is able to borrow more abroad.

An opposite imbalance would require the central bank to absorb foreign exchange, paying with home money, to keep its currency from strengthening against foreign currencies. In doing so—and thus financing and maintaining the country's excess of sales over purchases in foreign transactions—the central bank faces no limit as definite as the limit to its support of a weak home currency. It can *create* its home currency if necessary to keep it from strengthening and to pay for foreign exchange (or gold) bought; but a central bank in the opposite position cannot, of course, just create foreign money.

Nowadays, instead of holding their exchange rates absolutely rigid, most countries let them fluctuate in a range narrower than 1 percent on either side of parity. When practically everyone is confident that these "support limits" to the range of fluctuation will hold firm, private movements of funds will reduce the necessary scale of official intervention. When the home currency sinks almost to its lower support limit, speculators will realize that it cannot sink much further and that any change in its rate will be upward. In buying the home currency, they will help make their expectations come true. At the opposite extreme of the range, speculative sales of the home currency (purchases of foreign exchange) will reinforce the official intervention and reduce the amount needed to hold the exchange rate within the declared limits.

Speculators act quite differently when they seriously doubt that the exchange-pegging agency will succeed in maintaining these limits. If the home currency is under intense downward pressure and requires heroic support, the chance of its devaluation far outweighs any slight chance of its being revalued upward. (The terms "devaluation" and "upward revaluation" refer to deliberate changes in the level of exchange-rate pegging. When a distinction is intended, "depreciation" and "appreciation" refer to free-market movements in unpegged rates.) Speculators expecting a fall in the home currency and a rise in the price of foreign exchange face practically a "heads-I-win-tails-I-break-even" opportunity, since their possible loss if the official defense of the rate succeeds is slight in comparison with their gain if devaluation occurs. Speculative transactions then reinforce the ordinary transactions that may exhaust the central bank's foreign-exchange reserves and force devaluation. Even shifts in the timing of ordinary commercial payments (so-called "leads and lags") may come into play: merchants ordinarily wanting to sell foreign exchange for home currency will delay doing so, waiting for a possible devaluation, while merchants needing to buy foreign exchange will hasten to do so before a possible rise in its price in home currency.

Conversely, if people suspect that a currency under strong upward pressure will be revalued upward, speculators enjoy their so-called "one-way option" in the direction opposite to the one just described. "Leads and lags," similarly, work in the direction of hastening purchases and delaying sales of the strong currency, increasing the volume of official intervention necessary to stave off the expected upward revaluation.

In short, firm confidence in the declared narrow limits to exchange-rate fluctuation enlists private speculation in helping the central bank maintain those limits, but strong distrust works the other way and magnifies the central bank's task. The currency crises experienced since World War II, notably the crises of the pound sterling, reached the crisis stage precisely because devaluation of the currency under suspicion was considered a real possibility.

THE GOLD STANDARD

The international gold standard limited exchange-rate fluctuations before World War I in a way slightly different from the way typical now. Instead of regularly intervening directly on the foreign-exchange market, each government or central bank made its currency and gold freely interconvertible at a fixed price. The United States, for example, would coin gold into money and redeem money in gold at the rate of

$20.67 per ounce. The British pound sterling "contained" 4.8665 times as much gold as the dollar. When the dollar price of sterling rose above this "mint par" of $4.8665 by more than roughly two cents, arbitrageurs could make a profit. They would redeem dollars in gold, ship the gold to England, have the gold recoined there into pounds sterling (or sell it to the Bank of England at a corresponding price), thereby obtain sterling for dollars more cheaply than at the exchange rate, and sell the sterling on the foreign-exchange market for more dollars than they started with. In so doing, the gold arbitrageurs would check any further rise in the dollar rate on sterling. At the opposite extreme, when the dollar price of sterling fell more than roughly two cents below mint par, arbitrageurs could profitably redeem sterling in gold, ship the gold to the United States and convert it into dollars, thereby obtain more dollars for their sterling than corresponded to the exchange rate, and have a profit in dollars after buying back their original amount of sterling on the foreign-exchange market. By so doing, they would check any further fall in the dollar rate on sterling.

The spread between the mint par and each of the two so-called "gold points" on either side of it corresponded to the costs of crating and shipping and insuring the gold, the interest lost on wealth tied up in gold in transit, and other costs of carrying out the arbitrage. Since the interest loss and other costs of gold arbitrage changed from time to time and since some of the costs were matters of rough estimate anyway, the spread was not constant and precise. Still, the limits to exchange-rate fluctuation under the gold standard ordinarily stayed close to mint par, as our example suggests.

Before 1914, in short, each government typically left exchange-rate-stabilizing operations to private gold arbitrageurs. With only minor exceptions, it restrained itself to maintaining two-way convertibility between its monetary unit and a fixed amount of gold.

In those days, incidentally, the term "convertibility" meant the unrestricted redeemability of a currency in a fixed amount of gold. At present, with redeemability considered out of the question, at least for private holders of money, "convertibility" has been watered down to mean freedom from government restrictions on making payments with a currency and on selling it for foreign currencies. If only foreign holders but not domestic holders of a currency enjoy this freedom from restrictions on what they can do with it, the currency is said to possess "nonresident convertibility," which is a rather common condition nowadays.

When a gold-standard currency had weakened almost to its so-called gold export point, people would realize that it could not weaken much further and that it would probably rise. Speculative or quasi-speculative capital movements then came to the support of the currency and tended to keep gold exports from actually becoming profitable. At the other extreme, outflows of speculative capital from a country whose currency had almost reached its gold import point would tend to keep inward gold arbitrage from becoming profitable. The process was essentially the same as the one that operates when people are confident that exchange rates will remain officially pegged within declared limits. The danger of distrust and of destabilizing speculation was slighter under the gold standard than it sometimes is now because everyone realized that preserving two-way convertibility between each national money unit and a fixed quantity of gold was then almost an overriding goal of policy.

The permanence of this policy rested, in turn, on a connection between a country's monetary gold stock and its stock of all kinds of money, including banknotes and bank deposits. In a country losing gold because of excess imports of goods, services, and securities, the total money supply tended to shrink; a country gaining gold experienced monetary expansion. Even though countries are no longer on a real gold standard, a similar process tends to operate under the present-day system of fixed exchange rates. The appendix to Chapter 5 will explain this process and its importance more fully and will also describe how policy may either reinforce or neutralize it.

REFERENCES

1. PAUL EINZIG. *A Textbook on Foreign Exchange.* New York: St. Martin's Press, 1966.

2. ALAN R. HOLMES and FRANCIS H. SCHOTT. *The New York Foreign Exchange Market.* Federal Reserve Bank of New York, 1965.

3. GUENTER REIMANN and EDWIN F. WIGGLESWORTH. *The Challenge of International Finance.* New York: McGraw-Hill Book Company, 1966. (This large volume contains essays by many experts with a generally more practical than academic orientation.)

4. FRITZ MACHLUP. *International Payments, Debts, and Gold.* New York: Charles Scribner's Sons, 1964. Essay I.

5. ARTHUR I. BLOOMFIELD. *Monetary Policy under the International Gold Standard: 1880–1914.* Federal Reserve Bank of New York, 1959.

6. ROBERT TRIFFIN. *The Evolution of the International Monetary System: Historical Reappraisal and Future Perspectives.* International Finance Section, Princeton University, 1964.

3

BALANCE-OF-PAYMENTS

CONCEPTS

A balance of payments is a two-sided summary of a country's recorded or estimated international transactions during a year or other period. It covers not only transactions that directly give rise to supplies of and demands for currencies on the foreign-exchange market but other transactions also. To understand the concept, we must become acquainted with some accounting conventions and terminology. A grasp of the terminology is also essential for understanding descriptions of countries' international payments positions and theories of how the international monetary mechanism works. In international monetary economics, understanding the language and understanding the substance are closely interwoven.

CREDITS AND DEBITS

The two sides of a country's balance of payments are commonly labeled "receipts" and "payments," but this terminology is misleading. Neutral, technical language is safer: it reminds people that classifying transactions is a technical matter and warns them against thinking they understand more than they do. For this reason we shall label the two sides "plus" or "credit" and "minus" or "debit." The "plus" column lists commodity exports and other transactions of kinds ordinarily entailing payments from foreigners to residents of the home country and thus an exchange of foreign for home money. The "minus" column lists imports and other transactions ordinarily entailing payments from residents to foreigners and thus an exchange of home for foreign money. Each transaction appears in one list or the other according to which way payment for a transaction of that sort would *ordinarily* go, whether or not payment actually occurs in each individual case. Actual receipts of money do *not* belong in the misnamed "receipts" column, nor do payments of money belong in the "payments" column.

A commodity export ordinarily brings an inpayment from foreigners and so belongs on the "plus" or "credit" side of the balance of payments of the United States. The payment ordinarily entailed gives rise to a demand for dollars to be bought with foreign money, that is, a supply of foreign money to be sold for dollars. An export of goods still counts in the "plus" column even if the goods go abroad as a gift, or if they are sold on credit and will not be paid for until the following year. (The word "credit" as just used—referring to a loan granted in connection with selling goods—should of course not be confused with "credit" in the sense of a "plus" item in the balance of payments.) Goods exported still count in the "plus" column even if they will never be paid for in the event the foreign buyer defaults. Loans and gifts to foreigners count on the opposite side, the "minus" or "debit" or commodity-import side. The reason is that if they were made in money (which, for simplicity, we assume to be the "ordinary" procedure), the loans or gifts would entail exchanges of home for foreign money on the market. Loans and gifts still count this same way even if not made in cash, even if a loan takes the form of credit granted in a sale of merchandise or if a gift takes the form of merchandise. Settling an old debt owed to foreigners also counts on the "minus" side. (Just because the interpretation is so strained, it helps the memory to think of loans and gifts and repayments of debt to foreigners as imports of foreign IOU's and thank-you letters and our own cancelled IOU's; these imaginary imports of pieces of paper belong in the same column as imports of merchandise.)

Among loans to foreigners on the minus side of the United States balance of payments, increases in American accounts in foreign banks deserve special mention. After all, a bank deposit is traditionally regarded as a debt of the bank to its depositor, and an increase in American deposits in foreign banks does represent a "capital outflow" or "capital export." Acquiring a bank deposit abroad ordinarily would involve buying foreign exchange with dollars. (Making new loans and investments abroad, whether by acquiring bank deposits or other claims or properties, as well as reversing or paying off earlier foreign loans and investments in the United States, are all examples of capital export. Capital exports belong on the minus side of the United States balance of payments, along with commodity imports.) American acquisition of foreign paper money, just as of accounts in foreign banks, also represents a capital export, a loan to foreigners, since the paper money represents a claim on foreigners; in a perhaps fictitious sense, it is debt of the foreign issuers. Similarly, getting back American money previously held by foreigners counts as getting out of debt to foreigners, a capital export. In short, Americans' receipt of money paid by foreigners belongs on the minus or debit side of the balance of payments—the so-called *payments* rather than receipts side—which again illustrates how dangerous these popular terms are.

Similar items on the opposite side include increases in foreign-owned balances in American banks and decreases in American balances in foreign banks, as well as increases in foreign holdings of American currency and decreases in American holdings of foreign currency. These are all examples of "capital imports"; along with commodity exports, they count on the plus or credit side (the misleadingly so-called receipts side) of the American balance of payments.

Imports of gold for a country's official reserves and exports of gold from its reserves count on the minus and the plus sides, respectively, just like imports and exports of ordinary commodities. Gold, like commodities, ordinarily has to be paid for. If anyone drifts into thinking that minus transactions are "bad" but gold imports "good" and that plus transactions are "good" but gold exports "bad," that contradiction merely emphasizes the dangers of superficiality. Classifying balance-of-payments items is a technical matter.

In summary, let us list the sorts of transactions appearing on each side of the United States balance of payments. The plus or credit side includes transactions whose settlement *ordinarily entails* foreign payments to Americans and, consequently, exchanges of foreign money for dollars. They include American exports of goods and services to foreigners. (The services include the continuing foreign use of American capital previously lent or invested abroad, which ordinarily involves foreign payment of interest or dividends to Americans and is valued accordingly.) Other plus items are foreign gifts and other "unilateral transfers" received by Americans, capital imports through new loans and investments and bank deposits made in the United States by foreigners, capital imports through recovery by Americans of their loans and investments and bank accounts previously placed abroad, and exports of gold from the United States.

The minus or debit side includes transactions whose settlement *ordinarily entails* American payments to foreigners and thus exchanges of dollars for foreign money. They include American imports of goods and services from foreigners, including the currently-paid-for continuing services of foreign capital previously lent or invested in the United States. They also include American gifts and other "unilateral transfers" to foreigners, capital exports through new loans and investments and bank deposits made abroad by Americans, capital exports through recovery by foreigners of their loans and investments and bank accounts previously placed in the United States, and American imports of gold.

EQUALITY OF THE TWO TOTALS

As some of the examples suggest, particularly the examples of goods sold on credit or sent as a gift, every transaction has two aspects. (Strictly speaking, the word "transaction" as used so far meant *aspect* of a transaction.) The two aspects of each transaction are equal in amount but appear on opposite sides of the balance of payments. An American commodity export (a plus item) must be matched on the minus side somehow—by credit (a loan) extended to its foreign buyer, by a gift of its value to foreigners, by commodity imports accepted in a barter deal, by actually taking payment in American or foreign money (which means foreigners' disinvestment in American bank balances or currency they already held or Americans' investment in foreign bank balances or currency they newly acquire, either of which counts as an American "capital export"), or in some other way. The value of an American gift to foreigners appears on the minus side of the United States balance of payments, the side for aspects of transactions that, along with commodity imports, ordinarily entail outpayments, as the gift would do if made in money. The form in which the gift is transmitted, such as commodities exported, however, appears on the export or plus side. If the foreigners take and hold the gift in the form of American money, they are investing in a claim on the United States; and even this way of their accepting the gift counts as a plus for the United States. In effect, the country is borrowing back the value of its gift to foreigners: the money transferred to foreign ownership represents IOU's "exported" to them; the United States is "importing capital" from them.

Besides noting the two equal-and-opposite aspects of every transaction, there is a second way to see why the totals of the plus or credit items and of the minus or debit items must be equal. A country's people, businesses, and other economic units cannot buy goods and services worth more than those they sell unless they draw down their cash reserves (as of gold, foreign money, and bank accounts abroad), sell off some of their investments, obtain repayment of other debt owed to them, borrow (perhaps by obtaining credit when making purchases), or receive gifts or indemnities or the like. Conversely, a country's people, businesses, and other economic units cannot sell more worth of goods and services than they buy unless they engage in matching debit transactions by accumulating monetary reserves, investing, lending, paying off debt, or giving gifts or paying indemnities. Much the same is true of an individual family. Examples of credit items in a family's balance of payments might be: sales of goods or labor or professional services or of room and board to lodgers; earning of interest and dividends on bank accounts and securities and of profits on a family-owned business; receipt of gifts; new borrowing, such as obtaining credit in buying goods; reversing loans and investments made earlier, as by selling stocks and drawing down currency hoards and bank accounts; and selling gold coins from a collection. Opposite items on the debit side should be easy to think of. The family clearly cannot make current purchases of goods and services in excess of its sales without at the same time receiving gifts, borrowing, drawing down currency or bank balances, otherwise recovering old loans or selling off investments, or selling gold (perhaps coins or jewelry). Conversely, the family cannot earn more than it currently spends without lending, investing, making gifts, accumulating cash and bank accounts, and the like.

The necessary equality of debits and credits follows from sheer definitions and arithmetic and does not guarantee "equilibrium" in any reassuring sense of the word. Total credits would equal total debits even for a family or a country in dire straits.

Definitions of a balance of payments and of how its parts interlock admittedly seem paradoxical at first. Familiarity eventually makes everything seem consistent and even natural. Some actual figures for the United States, shown on page 34, will help. The main point to grasp, so far, is why the two sides add up to the same total amount. They would, anyway, if all the figures were complete and exact. Statisticians use a fudging item called *errors and omissions* to make the two sides equal, as in principle they must be. They must be equal for the same general reason that both sides of a company's balance sheet or income statement must: it follows from interlocking definitions.

DEFICITS AND SURPLUSES

What, then, could a balance-of-payments *deficit* mean? Before answering, we should notice the *principle of compensating balances:* if balance-of-payments items are grouped into two or more categories or "accounts," an excess of debits (or credits) in one or more of them must be matched by an equal but opposite total excess in the remaining ones. One way of grouping the items, for example, could set up the following accounts: Current Account (including goods-and-services trade and investment income), Unilateral Transfers (including private and government gifts, indemnities, and the like), Ordinary Capital Account (including the making of new and reversal of old foreign loans and investments in both directions, except for those classified under the final heading to be given in this list), Special Government Transactions (consisting of government transactions considered distinctive enough to deserve separate notice but not classified under the final heading), Errors and Omissions (the plus or minus figure included to fudge for incompleteness and inaccuracies in the other figures), and, finally, the Settlement Account (still to be described). Some of these accounts will show minus balances, others plus balances; but the totals of plus balances and of minus balances will be equal, making the total of all accounts zero.

By the very meaning of the Settlement Account, the items in all *other* accounts are considered "ordinary" (or relatively ordinary) transactions; they are grouped "above the line" that separates them from settlement transactions. A "deficit" in a country's balance of payments means an excess of minuses over pluses "above the line" matched by an excess of pluses "below the line"; the opposite imbalance is a "surplus." The size of a country's deficit or surplus depends on just how its various transactions are classified (on the location of "the line" between ordinary and settlement transactions), and this is a matter of judgment, not specified for all time in any hard and fast way.

In general, the transactions classified "above the line" are those supposedly undertaken for motives other than concern for the country's overall balance-of-payments position and the strength of its currency. Foreign travel undertaken for pleasure and imports and exports undertaken for profit are standard examples. Even most government transactions count as ordinary: overseas defense spending and foreign aid are examples, since their motives are military, political, or humanitarian. (Awkwardly enough, some special government transactions have been counted above the line in the balance-of-payments statistics of the United States for the past several years. Apparently, the purpose has been to make the United States deficit look smaller than it otherwise would, and the excuse has been that such transactions are more *nearly* ordinary, at least, than those counted below the line. The next chapter gives some further explanation.)

Below the line, the "compensatory" or "settlement" transactions are those supposedly undertaken to finance or settle any imbalance between the plus and minus totals of ordinary transactions. Characteristically, they are transactions carried out by the government or central bank to cope with the country's international payments position; more specifically, they are purchases and sales of gold and foreign exchange made to hold the value of the national currency steady on the foreign-exchange market. In addition, certain private capital movements may be counted below the line for at least two reasons. First, they may be considered subject to relatively great influence by interest-rate or other government policies adopted in view of the country's payments and currency position. Secondly, they may change the volume of indebtedness to foreigners of types that are considered in some sense to be claims on or offsets to the country's gold and foreign-exchange reserves. The problem of classifying capital movements above or below the line is complicated by the desire to have the country's deficit or surplus figure serve as a signal for necessary or desirable policies; hence, the purpose for which the figure is wanted and the degree of importance attributed to it affect the classification of doubtful transactions.

The figure reported for a country's deficit or surplus cannot be a definite, objective historical fact. One should beware of taking it too seriously and being misled by its meaning. The figure depends on where "the line" is drawn between settlement and ordinary transactions, and that depends largely on conjectured motives, on personal judgment, and on conventional and even rather arbitrary classifications of doubtful items.

In theorizing about balance-of-payments disequilibrium and adjustment, however, it is usually legitimate to ignore the fuzziness and arbitrariness unavoidable in work with actual figures. The deficits and surpluses contemplated in theoretical discussions are assumed to be too large to depend on fine points of classification. Equilibrium means the absence of a deficit or a surplus.

REFERENCES

1. J. E. MEADE. *The Balance of Payments*. London: Oxford University Press, 1951. Chapters I, II.

2. FRITZ MACHLUP. *International Payments, Debts, and Gold*. New York: Charles Scribner's Sons, 1964. Essays III, V, VI, VII.

4

THE UNITED STATES
BALANCE OF PAYMENTS

This chapter illustrates balance-of-payments concepts by applying them to the international transactions of the United States. Table 1 will help give definiteness to the abstract concepts. The United States payments position is also worth special attention because it raises instructive questions about the nature of balance-of-payments disequilibrium, because it illustrates the policy expedients often adopted to deal with payments problems, and because the dollar holds a prominent place in the working of the existing international monetary system and in diagnoses of the need for reform.

THE "LIQUIDITY" DEFICIT

In the statistics of most countries, the below-the-line financing that matches and settles any deficit on account of ordinary transactions consists of a decline of official reserves of gold and foreign exchange, together with any official borrowing abroad used to supplement drafts on these reserves. (Members of the International Monetary Fund are increasingly coming to count their "gold tranche" positions in the Fund as parts of their official reserves; see pages 99–100.) A surplus is settled by the growth of official reserves and the repayment of official foreign indebtedness. The classification of transactions is more complicated for the United States, since many foreign countries hold dollars in their official reserves. For some years the statisticians in the U. S. Department of Commerce have defined the financing of a deficit in the United States balance of payments as a loss of official gold and foreign-exchange reserves to foreigners plus any rise in foreign holdings of quickly cashable claims on the United States. These liquid claims include bank accounts, bankers' acceptances and Treasury bills and other kinds of money-market paper, and marketable or convertible United States government obligations of all maturities (because of their ready marketability, even long-term government bonds are considered to be liquid claims). Changes in claims held by private foreigners count just the same as changes in claims held by foreign official agencies.

A deficit or surplus settled in the way just described is called the "Liquidity Balance" in United States international transactions. This Liquidity concept admittedly treats flows of short-term private capital in an asymmetrical way: changes in United States liquid liabilities to private foreigners go below the line, while changes in private United States claims on foreigners go above. Suppose that a United States commercial bank acquires a £1000 balance in an English bank and gives it a $2400 (= £1000) balance in return. The first part of the transaction counts above the line as an outflow of U. S. capital, worsening the United States deficit, while the inflow of English capital counts below the line as a settlement item. On the Liquidity concept, this swapping of bank accounts swells the United States deficit by $2400!

The excuse for this asymmetry is that United States liquid liabilities even to private foreigners are a potential claim on the United States gold stock: they may readily be transferred to foreign central banks or governments, to whom the United States will sell gold on demand. But private United States claims on foreigners count above the line because they are not readily available to the United States authorities as reserves with which to support the dollar on the foreign-exchange market. Far from being arbitrary, the asymmetry reflects the real world. Because the dollar, unlike most other currencies, serves as a reserve currency throughout the world, the United States should compare its official reserve assets with all its liquid liabilities, those owed by and to private parties as well as those owed by and to official agencies. The Liquidity concept of deficit or surplus focuses attention both on the reserves available to the United States authorities to defend the foreign-exchange value of the dollar and on the liquid claims that foreigners may exercise against these reserves.

In other words, an inflow of foreign private short-term funds matching a deficit on other items in the balance of payments may be cause for concern because it sets the stage for possible withdrawal later. Although private holders cannot directly redeem their dollars in gold at the United States Treasury, they could hasten to sell them for other currencies on the ordinary foreign-exchange market. Foreign central banks, to keep their own currencies from strengthening against the dollar in violation of the policy of fixed exchange rates, would absorb the abnormal offerings of dollars. As official holders, the foreign central banks could then redeem the dollars in gold. But if this is the worry, why should we distinguish foreign holdings of government securities and short-term claims so sharply from foreign holdings of corporate stocks and bonds? Efforts to sell these securities and take home the proceeds could be just as disruptive. Even more potentially disruptive, because of the larger amounts of money involved, would be an attempted run out of *American*-owned liquid assets and securities for fear of devaluation of the dollar. It does not matter much whether foreigners or Americans exchange dollar assets for foreign currencies. In either case, the dollars acquired by foreign authorities in their exchange-stabilization operations become eligible for redemption in gold.

The Liquidity concept of the United States deficit is often criticized for not adequately recognizing the positive reasons why foreigners acquire dollar claims. It does not fully appreciate why the United States money market is so attractive to foreigners as a place to invest liquid funds and hold working balances. Foreigners need dollar balances for international transactions just as Americans need dollar balances for domestic transactions. Another sizable portion of private foreign claims may be linked closely to foreign debts to Americans; so these claims, also, are unlikely to be withdrawn. To treat flows of foreign private capital as different from flows of United States private capital or as similar to flows of foreign official capital thus exaggerates the United States deficit and the threat to the nation's gold stock.

For reasons partly related to this criticism, some economists deplore the practice of counting American long-term lending and investing in Europe toward a United States deficit while counting European lending and investing in short-term claims on the United States not toward avoiding but toward precariously financing the deficit. In the American balance-of-payments position, correctly understood, these flows of American long-term capital and European short-term capital largely offset each other. They represent constructive exchanges motivated by a generally stronger desire of Europeans than of Americans to place their savings at short term and do their borrowing at long term. The greater competitiveness and efficiency of American than European financial institutions and the greater size of the market they serve also promote the offsetting capital flows. From this view, the money and capital markets of the United States serve as a gigantic financial intermediary for the world; they adapt the characteristics of claims and debts to the different preferences of lenders and borrowers. Part of the reported outflows of capital from the United States, therefore, may not represent any intended net transfer of capital in the form of real goods and services. Instead, these outflows arise from the intermediary role of the United States in enabling foreigners to acquire short-term assets by incurring long-term debt or by transferring ownership claims to American investors. Just as financial intermediation within a country aids capital formation and growth even though the institutions themselves may not be ultimate providers of resources, so flows of capital into and out of the United States may aid capital formation and growth abroad, even apart from any real transfer of capital in the form of goods and services. To some extent, even central banks may count among the

Europeans who actively want to acquire short-term dollar assets. So far as a genuine foreign demand for liquid dollar holdings offsets the outflow of long-term capital from the United States, no pressure occurs against the dollar on the foreign-exchange market. Not everything that counts as a balance-of-payments deficit nowadays is necessarily a true disequilibrium requiring correction.

THE DEFICIT MEASURED BY OFFICIAL RESERVE TRANSACTIONS

After a government-appointed committee of experts (the Bernstein Committee) issued its report in 1965, the United States began publishing figures arranged according to a second concept of deficit or surplus. This "Official Reserve Transactions" concept, like the Liquidity concept, measures the settlement of an overall deficit or surplus by what has happened to United States reserves and to certain types of claims against the United States. Both count any change in the sum of United States monetary gold, United States official holdings of convertible foreign currencies, and the United States gold tranche in the International Monetary Fund as an increase or a decrease in reserves. The difference comes in the classification of foreign claims on the United States. The Liquidity concept puts changes in these claims above or below the line according to their status as long-term or short-term claims; the Official Reserve Transactions (ORT) concept puts the changes above or below the line according to whether the claims belong to private foreigners or to foreign authorities.

The ORT concept thus treats any increase in foreign private claims on the United States, whether liquid or illiquid, as an ordinary capital inflow. In treating movements of foreign and American short-term capital alike, it recognizes the distinction between private transactions and transactions of monetary authorities. It also recognizes that satisfying the normally growing desire of private foreigners for dollar holdings should not count as measuring and settling a United States deficit. It recognizes that movements of short-term as well as long-term capital owned by private foreigners (including individuals and commercial banks and other businesses) generally reflect personal and business motives and so differ in character from the transactions of United States and foreign monetary authorities. The ORT concept focuses attention on the dollar claims that foreign monetary authorities have acquired or disposed of, usually in maintaining the parities of their currencies.

Unlike the Liquidity concept, the ORT concept recognizes the artificiality of distinguishing between liquid United States liabilities and certain nonliquid United States liabilities to foreign authorities. It puts changes in both below the line. The decision on which nonliquid liabilities are to be handled that way is admittedly somewhat arbitrary. The ones in question consist chiefly of nonmarketable, nonconvertible United States government securities held by foreign authorities.

According to the Bernstein Committee, the rationale of the ORT presentation of the figures is that a summary indicator of the balance of payments is wanted because central banks and treasuries are responsible for maintaining stable exchange rates. To carry out this responsibility, these authorities settle the net deficits and surpluses arising from all other international transactions by gaining or losing reserve assets and by increasing or decreasing their liabilities to foreign monetary authorities. The size of an authority's transactions both in its own reserves and in its liabilities held as reserves by foreign authorities supposedly measures the scale of market intervention necessary to maintain exchange stability.

Critics of the ORT concept note that its distinction between private and official holdings of dollar claims can itself be rather artificial. In many foreign countries, central banks manipulate the dollar holdings of commercial banks. The Liquidity measure of the United States deficit, on the other hand, is not affected by policy-induced shifts of dollar claims between central and commercial banks, since changes in all foreign liquid claims go below the line anyway. No clear line separates foreign dollar holdings that do from those that do not stand as offsets to the gold and foreign-exchange reserves of the United States.

The arguments for and against the Liquidity and ORT concepts of imbalance illustrate what we have been insisting on all along: there is no single unambiguously best measure of a country's international payments position. Those two measures are mere clues about equilibrium and disequilibrium. Deficits and surpluses are not definite things objectively existing in the real world and waiting to be described with precision. When one financial writer told the Bernstein Committee, "All I want is one number, with no if's, but's, or maybe's," he was asking the impossible.

OTHER MEASURES OF IMBALANCE

Government publications now report both the Liquidity and the Official Reserve Transactions figures of the United States deficit. Still other concepts have sometimes been used. The concept of *basic balance* or *basic deficit* was popular a few years ago. It avoided the Liquidity concept's asymmetrical treatment of foreign and American short-term capital movements by putting both below the line (whereas the ORT concept puts both above, so far as privately owned capital is concerned). The concept of basic deficit kept below the line not only the traditional settlement items but also movements of United States short-term capital, commercial credits received by Americans from foreigners, and errors and omissions. Transactions in these categories were supposedly more volatile and less meaningful than the "basic" transactions in goods and services, foreign aid, and long-term capital. Since the basic deficit was often smaller than the Liquidity deficit, the Administration understandably preferred that concept. Various concepts of *deficit on "regular" transactions* (as distinguished from special transactions) have also been used or suggested. They tend to give a less cheerful impression of the recent United States payments position because they put below the line certain special official transactions (notably, advance repayments of debts owed to the United States government by foreign governments) designed to lessen resort to other ways of financing a deficit on ordinary transactions.

The conceptual difficulties just reviewed are not the only reason for skepticism about published figures on the United States payments position. Regardless of their arrangement, the figures themselves suffer from inaccuracies and incompleteness.

THE BALANCE OF PAYMENTS IN 1966

Table 1 summarizes the figures for the United States in 1966. To gain facility in using and rearranging balance-of-payments statistics, the reader should consult the more detailed figures in the sources listed at the end of this chapter.

TABLE 1

THE UNITED STATES BALANCE OF PAYMENTS, 1966

(millions of dollars)

	Plus Items	Minus Items
Merchandise trade	29,168	25,510
Military sales and expenditures	847	3,694
Income on private and government investments	6,245	2,074
Other services	6,779	6,659
Remittances and pensions, net		1,010
United States private long-term capital flow, net		3,719
United States private short-term capital flow, net		413
United States government grants and capital flow, net		3,446
Foreign capital flow, net (excluding changes in liquid assets in the United States)	2,512	
Errors and omissions		383
	45,551	46,908
Excess of minus-over-plus items so far = balance on the Liquidity concept		1,357
Decline in United States reserves (gold, convertible currencies, and gold tranche in IMF)	568	
Decline in liquid liabilities to foreign official holders (including IMF)		1,595
Increase in liquid liabilities to other foreign holders (private holders and international organizations other than IMF)	2,384	
Excess of below-the-line plus over minus items = settlement of the Liquidity deficit	1,357	

As the reader should verify by doing the additions and subtractions himself, the excess of minus over plus items above the line equals the excess of plus over minus items below the line: $1,357 million. This figure measures the United States deficit according to the Liquidity concept.

Several rearrangements will convert the presentation to the ORT concept. A net plus item of $802 million of changes in certain *non-liquid* United States liabilities to foreign official holders (that is, an increase in United States indebtedness) is concealed in the net figures on government and foreign capital shown above the line in the table. We now shift this amount below the line. At the same time, we shift the net plus figure of $2,384 million for changes in liquid liabilities to nonofficial foreign holders from below to above the line. These two shifts add a net plus of $1,582 million to the above-the-line figures, changing the net minus balance there to a net plus of $225 million. Below the line, as settlement of this ORT surplus and totaling −$225 million, we now have +$568 million of change (decrease) in United States reserves, +$802 million of change (increase) in nonliquid liabilities to foreign official holders, and −$1,595 million of change (decrease) in liquid liabilities to foreign official holders.

The unusual but small United States surplus on the ORT concept in 1966 reflected an extraordinary buildup of foreign private holdings of dollar assets. Relatively high interest rates and bearishness on sterling during the summer were among the influences affecting capital movements. By coincidence, the Liquidity and ORT deficits had been almost the same—$1,335 and $1,304 million, respectively—in 1965, when private foreign holdings of liquid dollar assets grew much less than usual. Over the seven years 1960–1966, the deficits totaled about 27 percent less on the ORT basis than on the Liquidity basis. This difference averaged $641 million a year.

DEVELOPMENT OF THE UNITED STATES
PAYMENTS POSITION

The United States has been running a deficit every year from 1950 on, except 1957. But apart from the $3.5 billion recorded in 1950 under the influences of the Korean conflict and the devaluations of many foreign currencies the year before, the deficits had been moderate. From 1951 through 1956 they averaged only $1.2 billion a year on the Liquidity basis. The return from a surplus of $0.6 billion in 1957 to a deficit of $3.4 billion in 1958 reflected a return of world trade to normal after reopening of the Suez Canal.

It also reflected a change in the character of the deficit. Until around 1958, the United States wanted to help foreign countries recover from the war and rebuild their gold and foreign-exchange reserves in preparation for making their currencies convertible. (Convertibility was explained on page 15.) The United States deficits and even substantial foreign purchases of gold caused little worry. Rather than seen as contributing toward any problem of a U. S. deficit, United States foreign aid and to some extent U. S. overseas military expenditures during this period were seen as helping remedy the reserve shortage of foreign countries.

Any balance-of-payments worries during this period centered, in fact, on a supposedly chronic and almost intractable "dollar shortage." With hindsight, it could be traced back several decades. Most of the world outside North America supposedly suffered from a persistent or recurrent tendency to spend more than it earned (or borrowed at long term) in dealing with North America. Its reserves of gold and dollars seemed in continual danger of running out unless bolstered by controls over trade and payments and by resort to loans or grants from the United States or American-financed international agencies. Writings on the supposed dollar shortage kept piling up even in the late 1950s, years after the gold and dollar reserves of foreign countries as a whole had begun a sustained rise and right up to the time when the fashion reversed itself into worry about an American *deficit* and a dollar *glut*.

This happened around 1958. That year the United States Liquidity deficit of $3.4 billion was settled by an increase in short-term liabilities to foreigners and by an all-time record gold loss of $2.3 billion, about 10 percent of the gold stock at the beginning of the year. At the end of the year, newly flush with gold and dollars, Western Europe returned to external currency convertibility. The reappearance of heavy foreign borrowing in New York then joined the continuing international burdens of the United States in swelling the deficit further. On the Liquidity concept it reached almost $3.9 billion in both 1959 and 1960. (In October 1960, semispeculative capital outflows were dramatized by a brief sharp rise in the price of gold on the London market.) The yearly deficit averaged 74 percent larger over the nine years 1958–1966 than over the seven years 1950–1956. This contrast stands, even though the deficit shrank to an average of $2.1 billion on the Liquidity basis in 1961–1966. (Over the same six years the ORT deficit averaged $1.5 billion.) The improvement after 1960 is attributable partly to special transactions between the United States and foreign governments (partly intended, no doubt, to make the figures look better).

THE SHAPE OF THE RECENT DEFICIT

Looking unanalytically at the bare figures and glossing over year-to-year changes, we can resolve the United States deficit into military expenditures overseas, government aid grants, and net outflows of government and private capital totaling more than a surplus of earnings over expenditures in commodity trade, income on foreign investments, and transactions in some services. (Not all services, though, yield net earnings. Receipts from foreign tourists, for example, fall far short of spending abroad by American tourists.) The large surplus in goods and services trade suggests that the overall deficit does not reflect any tendency for Americans to live beyond their means. Nor is the United States incurring any net debt to foreigners or using up its international capital. On the contrary, United States ownership of assets abroad continues to grow faster than foreign ownership of investments in and claims on the United States. At the end of 1965, estimated American long- and short-term foreign investments totaled twice as much as, or $61 billion more than, foreign investments in the United States. Only the United States liquid reserve position is being impaired. (By April 1967 the official United States figure on liquid liabilities to foreigners was more than twice as large as the nation's gold stock and eight times as large as the "free gold" in excess of the legally required backing for paper money in circulation.)

Of course, transactions interact. If the net minuses on military, aid, and capital accounts had been smaller than they were, the goods-and-services surplus would also have been smaller. And anyway, equilibrium does not require balance in each separate category of a country's international transactions. As compared with blaming the particular categories in deficit, it might not be much more unreasonable to blame some of the surplus categories for not being still larger. It might not be entirely illogical to put some blame even on growing surplus categories for not growing still more. Furthermore, even if we could be sure about the causes of the overall deficit, they would not necessarily coincide with the conditions that "ought" to be eliminated to restore equilibrium.

If space permitted and if we guarded against wrongly supposing that we were thereby learning the causes of the United States deficit, it would be instructive to survey the changes in major categories of United States transactions in recent years. The make-up as well as the size of the overall deficit has varied sharply. Some items have improved from one year to the next while others have worsened— sometimes trade in goods and services, sometimes long-term and sometimes short-term capital movements. The surplus on goods-and-services account fell as low as $147 million in 1959, rose as high as $8.5 billion in 1964, and then, under the influence of strong aggregate demand in the United States, dropped to $6.9 billion in 1965 and $5.1 billion in 1966. Thanks partly to changed international interest-rate relations and to liberalization of European controls, the net recorded outflow of capital from the United States shrank in 1959 and held the increase in the overall Liquidity deficit from the year before to about one-half billion dollars. (*Unrecorded* capital flows are generally thought to make up a large part of the "errors and omissions" item.) In 1960 the Liquidity deficit grew very slightly further as the capital account worsened while the merchandise trade balance recovered strongly. In 1964, when the current account was unusually strong, the net recorded outflow of private United States long- and short-term capital swelled to $6.5 billion.

POLICY EXPEDIENTS

This outflow of private capital had much to do with President Johnson's decision, early in 1965, to impose on banks and other businesses a program of "voluntary restraint" on their lending and investing abroad. In the judgment of some expert observers, ironically, a feeling that some such controls were in prospect had had a lot to do with the great spurt of capital outflow in the last few months of 1964.

The "voluntary restraint" helped cause a marked change in the structure of the balance of payments in 1965 and 1966. Its effects mingled with those of tight money and rising interest rates in the United States and with the effects of the Interest Equalization Tax on Americans' purchases of foreign securities. (That tax had been enacted in September 1964 with application retroactive to July 1963. In effect, it increases the interest cost to foreigners of borrowing in the United States. In February 1965 the tax was extended to long-term bank loans.) The net recorded outflow of private United States long- and short-term capital shrank by $2.8 billion between 1964 and 1965 and recovered by only $0.4 billion in 1966. This shrinkage helped offset the decline of the trade surplus and the rise of Vietnam expenditures; the over-all deficit on both the Liquidity and ORT concepts shrank to $1.3 billion in 1965 (a figure smaller than that year's gold loss).

In 1966, as already mentioned, the ORT balance registered a small surplus, thanks to an extraordinary attraction of foreign private funds. The Liquidity deficit, however, widened slightly from the year before. Among other influences, imports of capital goods surged in 1966 as United States buyers turned increasingly to foreign suppliers for prompt delivery. The extent of overall deterioration was concealed by a variety of special official transactions, including debt prepayments and purchases of nominally nonliquid United States obligations by foreign and international authorities. Without those special transactions, the United States Liquidity deficit in 1966 would probably have been about $1 billion larger than reported. Once again we see why figures on balance-of-payments deficits and surpluses must be viewed with extreme skepticism. The principles of international monetary economics deserve more attention than figures supposedly describing recent history.

The gloomy balance-of-payments prospects for 1967 led the Administration to tighten the program of "voluntary restraint" on capital outflows and to raise the rate of the Interest Equalization Tax under authority of a new amendment. Even so, the payments position developed worse than had been expected. According to preliminary estimates, the Liquidity deficit reached nearly $4 billion in 1967, running at an annual rate of around $9 billion in the fourth quarter. The British devaluation of November 18 had apparently spurred outflows of capital from the United States.

In January 1968 the President made restrictions on business foreign investment mandatory (claiming authority under the Trading with the Enemy Act of 1917), tightened the still supposedly "voluntary" restrictions on foreign lending by financial institutions, asked Americans "temporarily" to forgo travel outside the Western Hemisphere (and asked Congress for legislation to encourage compliance), and proposed tax adjustments to discourage imports and promote exports.

The great attention that policy-makers have been giving to the capital account in recent years does not necessarily mean that the real source of United States payments difficulties lies here. United States foreign investments have contributed much not only to the large surplus of United States over foreign earnings on foreign loans and investments but also to the strength of domestic exports and of such other items as royalty earnings. Income remitted from private American direct investments abroad actually forms the second largest plus item, after merchandise exports, in the United States balance of payments. The annual excess of these remittances over the net capital outflow to expand direct investments exceeded $1 billion in every year from 1961 through 1964 and amounted to about $0.6 billion in 1965. Long-continued restrictions on United States investment abroad are likely to hamper earning and remitting profits. A corporation forced to restrict its overseas activities is likely in time to lose competitive ground in world markets.

Besides taxing and otherwise restricting capital outflows, the United States has tried many *ad hoc* expedients to cope with its payments problem. These expedients include the "tying" of foreign aid to its expenditure in the United States, as well as other export-promotion schemes, discouragements to imports such as cuts in the duty-free allowance for purchases brought home by returning American tourists, efforts to lure foreign tourists to the United States while encouraging Americans to "see America first," and a tightened ban on American ownership of gold. The United States has been trying to hold down overseas military expenditures by reducing various categories of overseas construction and administrative personnel, by exercising moral dissuasion against private spending by United States troops and dependents overseas, and by requiring American forces overseas to procure materials and supplies in the United States even if costs here are as much as 50 percent greater than locally (which, of course, inflates the dollar size of the defense budget). The United States has been pressuring foreign governments to carry bigger shares of the common defense and foreign-aid burdens not merely in the name of fairness but also for balance-of-payments reasons. Furthermore, the United States has asked them to order American military goods and pay in advance, or to repay debt ahead of schedule, or to acquire special nonnegotiable bonds instead of gold. The measures announced and proposed in January 1968 further substantially restrict how

Americans may use their dollars for investment, for travel, and possibly for imports. Restrictions on its usability are a very real cut in the *value* of the dollar. The discriminatory and unavowed character of this devaluation hardly makes it any more palatable. Ironically enough, the measures that add up to piecemeal devaluation are still being urged for *defense* of the dollar's value. Domestic monetary-fiscal policy has also felt the influence of the balance of payments; one example is the dubious effort begun in 1961 to "twist" the structure of interest rates to hold interest-sensitive funds in the United States.

The great changeability of the components of the United States balance of payments illustrates how international transactions can react sensitively not only to policy expedients but also to slight differences among countries in rates of economic growth and price inflation and perhaps interest, to changes in so-called "structural" conditions, and to special historical circumstances. A trade surplus or deficit is a difference between differences, since imports and exports are themselves differences between domestic production and domestic use of goods of the kinds traded. Forecasts can be little better than short-run extrapolations. A sensible policy would not have to rely on them.

The volatility of a balance of payments is not the same thing as an alternation of deficits and surpluses around a longer-run equilibrium. In the absence of quasi-automatic adjustment processes such as the next chapter describes, balance-of-payments troubles are likely to persist or recur. Instead of vanishing, they are likely, at best, to give old victims a respite as they turn to plague new ones. We should remember how fashionable the worry about a supposedly chronic and almost intractable "dollar shortage" remained until it gave way to the opposite worry about a stubborn United States deficit.

It is ironic how so small a deficit—always under one half of 1 percent of the gross national product from 1961 on—should cause so much worry and so much interference with the domestic and international policies Americans desire on other grounds. Even if the United States deficit were to vanish of its own accord or be cured in some acceptable way, problems would remain if no deeper reform accompanied this change. Largely because of the dollar's role as an international reserve currency, the conditions of the United States balance of payments and of the whole international monetary system are linked together. Curing the deficit would cut off the largest source of postwar growth in the "international liquidity" of foreign countries. The problem of the United States deficit thus blends in with the more general issue of world monetary reform, a topic considered in Chapters 7 through 10.

REFERENCES

1. U. S. DEPARTMENT OF COMMERCE. *Survey of Current Business.* Monthly. For balance-of-payments information, see the March, June, September, and December issues especially.

2. INTERNATIONAL MONETARY FUND. *Balance of Payments Yearbook.* Issued in loose-leaf installments.

3. CHARLES P. KINDLEBERGER. *Balance-of-Payments Deficits and the International Market for Liquidity.* Essay No. 46; International Finance Section, Princeton University, 1965.

4. WALTER S. SALANT. "Capital Markets and the Balance of Payments of a Financial Center." In William Fellner and others, *Maintaining and Restoring Balance in International Payments,* Princeton University Press, 1966, pp. 177–196.

5. REVIEW COMMITTEE FOR BALANCE OF PAYMENTS STATISTICS (Bernstein Committee). *The Balance of Payments Statistics of the United States.* Washington,, D. C.: Government Printing Office, 1965.

6. THOMAS E. DAVIS. "Measuring a Deficit or Surplus in the U. S. Balance of Payments." Federal Reserve Bank of Kansas City. *Monthly Review,* September-October 1966, pp. 14–18.

7. *The Dollar and the World Monetary System.* New York: Committee for Economic Development, 1966.

5

CORRECTION OF IMBALANCES

INDIVIDUAL AND NATIONAL
BALANCES OF PAYMENTS

The very existence of balance-of-payments troubles seems paradoxical when we reflect that a country's balance-of-payments position with the rest of the world is the total of the individual positions of all the persons or families, companies, and other private and government organizations composing the national economy. Each family and other unit can be regarded as having a balance of payments with everyone else, fellow citizens and foreigners lumped together. Any deficit for the country as a whole means that deficits outweigh surpluses in these individual positions. We expect the ordinary motivations of people to keep them from developing alarming deficits, that is, from running their assets down or their short-term debts up to an alarming extent. Even reckless persons would find their deficits limited by the sizes of their bank accounts and the limited willingness of others to go on making risky loans to them. How, then, can the country as a whole be in balance-of-payments trouble if its people are experiencing no such trouble?

The answer must be that something is interfering with the adjustment processes that would otherwise work through ordinary private motives. (There may be good reasons for interference; we shall not prejudge that issue here.) To understand what aspects of the interfering policies are crucial, we must understand how adjustment processes ideally would work. In the theoretical discussion that follows, we need not worry about precise definitions of deficit, surplus, and equilibrium; the rough-and-ready distinction between ordinary transactions and settlement transactions (perhaps including official exchange stabilization) is enough. (Remember: A deficit simply could not exist unless it were being financed somehow.) To simplify the explanation without changing the principles involved, we may even suppose that imports and exports of goods and services are the only kinds of ordinary transactions that take place. Balance or imbalance in "trade" thus coincides with balance or imbalance on account of all above-the-line transactions. (Alternatively, we could broaden the terms "imports" and "exports" to include not only purchases and sales of goods and services, even counting travel and the capital "services" for which interest and dividends are paid, but also lending and repaying, borrowing and receiving repayment, and all the other ordinary items on the two sides of the balance of payments.)

We shall focus our attention on deficits, or on disturbances that would cause them unless balancing processes were at work. A surplus can be troublesome for a country in its own way, but it is less likely to pose a crisis than a deficit is. To clinch his understanding, the reader should reason out for himself how to reverse our analysis to explain the correction of a surplus.

TYPES OF CORRECTION

A balance-of-payments deficit may cure itself "automatically" (through market incentives, that is, rather than by direct orders from some authority) in any of three ways. Each involves a fall in the ratio of total home to total foreign money income. Of course, no one makes decisions by watching this ratio; mentioning it is just a convenient way of organizing a comparison of the adjustment processes. First, home income could fall through a shrinkage in the physical volume of goods and services produced, with prices and wages unchanged. Secondly, the ratio could conceivably fall without any decline in home production and employment: home money income could fall simply through cuts in the prices and wages at which goods and services were valued. Thirdly, the ratio could fall through a change in the exchange rate that makes home and foreign money incomes comparable. Or the ratio could fall through a mix of changes in real income produced, prices and wages, and exchange rates.

Which mechanism or combination operates depends on the monetary relations among countries. Under a gold standard or other system that makes fixed exchange rates a dominant goal of domestic monetary and fiscal policy, the first and the second mechanisms operate together. Their relative importance depends on how frictionlessly prices and wages adjust down and up. If independent national fiat moneys are free to fluctuate against one another, the third mechanism operates.

ADJUSTMENT THROUGH INCOME AND PRICE LEVELS

We may understand the first two mechanisms working together by considering transactions between a single state (for example, Virginia) and the rest of the United States or of the world. Suppose a deficit develops. (To avoid contradicting arithmetic, we must allow some nonofficial below-the-line financing, after all: people can spend somewhat more than they currently earn by drawing down their bank accounts or going into debt.) Suppose either that the out-of-state demand for Virginia's apples and tobacco falls off or that some Virginian demand shifts from local to out-of-state goods. Either way, some Virginians see their incomes fall. They cut their own spending and so cut the incomes of other Virginians. Meanwhile, net transfers of money to outsiders (or loans from them) finance the trade deficit. With their incomes fallen and their holdings of cash or other financial assets shrunken or their debts swollen, Virginians cut down their buying from each other and from outsiders alike. Reduced business at home also spurs efforts to make sales outside the state. Virginia's imports and exports tend toward balance again at a new level. If the original disturbance were large and the correctives feebler and slower than they are in reality, still another aspect of adjustment would become noticeable. As net outpayments made Virginians less willing to buy and more eager to sell goods and services, prices and costs would fall. Some people both in and out of Virginia would switch some of their buying away from out-of-state goods to the relatively cheapened Virginia goods. The price-and-cost decline would affect mainly services and other "local" goods in which, by their very nature, interstate and international trade is relatively inactive (labor, haircuts, and houses are standard examples). Actively traded goods would be affected less because their prices are determined primarily by national and international supply and demand. Thus, local goods would fall in price relative to goods of kinds actively imported and exported; import-and-export-type goods would rise in price *relatively*. Consumers would have an incentive to switch their buying away from imports, while producers would have an incentive to switch their production or sales efforts to export goods.

The fall in Virginia's money income during correction of the deficit does not *necessarily* mean a fall in employment and production. If wages and the prices of local goods fall flexibly enough to bear the entire brunt of the disturbance and make resources shift among occupations, total production and employment can remain at their old levels. (The mix of products changes, but total production need not fall unambiguously.) A fall in money income would then correspond to a fall in the prices that translate real production into money income. The adjustment mechanism would be entirely of the second of the types listed above. In reality, though, prices and wages are not so completely flexible. They sink only stickily. A fall in money income corresponds partly to a fall in employment and production as well as in prices. With their real incomes reduced, people cut their purchases of imports and of exportable goods as well as of local goods. In reality, this first of the adjustment mechanisms listed combines with the second. It is an unpleasant and inefficient method of adjustment.

Cash balances and other financial-asset holdings play a role in the combined mechanism. Their shrinkage (as well as any growth of debt to outsiders) both finances the deficit while it lasts and helps correct it by restraining spending. In part, Virginians cut their spending on imports directly. Indirectly, by spending less on each other's goods and services, they bring the real-income and price effects of the adjustment process into play.

A deficit may be partly financed for a while in several semiautomatic ways, avoiding harsh and rapid correction through changes in production, employment, prices, wages, and holdings of money. To a large extent, goods are bought and sold on credit and not paid for for several weeks or months. The residents of a state or country with an excess of imports over exports are therefore obtaining loans almost automatically in connection with their excess purchases. Another cushioning effect is likely to work through interest rates. An import surplus implies expenditure in excess of current income, that is, investment spending in excess of saving. (See the section on the "absorption approach" later in this chapter.) As a result, interest rates are likely to rise in the deficit state or country, discouraging loans to outsiders while attracting loans from them. For example, the banks are likely to meet local demands for credit partly by selling some securities from their portfolios on the national or international market, thereby bringing capital into their region. The tighter the economic and financial integration is between the deficit region and the rest of the country or world, the more readily do these cushioning flows of capital respond to interest-rate differentials. Under the gold standard before 1914, national monetary authorities sometimes supplemented spontaneous tendencies by deliberate interest-rate policy; and under the present-day system of fixed exchange rates, such policies are still sometimes used to affect capital movements so as to help accommodate imbalances in payments. Of course, trade-related and interest-motivated flows of capital provide merely temporary finance for deficits; they cushion the corrective process but do not eliminate the need for it. The rise of interest rates in a deficit region may even make some slight contribution to the correction by tending to restrain aggregate demand for home and foreign goods and services alike.

THE GOLD STANDARD

For a very few decades before 1914, most major countries were on an international gold standard. Although their currencies were not as closely linked then as the dollars used in Virginia and the other forty-nine states are now, the link was fairly close. The link would be complete under the imaginary system in which gold coins were the only kind of money used in all countries. Their movement out of countries with balance-of-payments deficits into countries with surpluses would play the same role in adjustment as the movement of dollars between Virginia and the other states. A gold standard of the historical type works less surely and automatically than this, since each country's money supply consists not of gold alone but of paper money and bank deposits pyramided onto a fractional reserve of gold. No longer do money and gold coincide; rather, the redeemability of money in gold links the two together. When a country is running a balance-of-payments deficit, the foreigners will want payment in their own money or in the gold with which to get it. The money-redeeming authorities of the deficit country must supply the gold. And since their gold reserve is only a fraction of their country's total money supply, the gold may run out before the deficit corrects itself. This danger spells balance-of-payments trouble for the country, even though its people, as individuals, may feel no particular trouble. The country's trouble ties in with official below-the-line transactions of the kind we have so far assumed away in explaining the automatic balancing process. Drawing on official reserves to keep the currency's value tied to gold makes up these settlement transactions.

Even under a fractional-reserve gold standard, the adjustment processes of the Virginia example *may,* after all, work powerfully and swiftly enough to cure a deficit before the country's gold is all gone. Imports and exports may balance themselves more or less adequately, most of the time, even though the linkage between the money supplies of different countries is far from rigid. But the looser the linkage, the greater the danger of balance-of-payments trouble. To play perfectly safe, the monetary authorities must allow or cause the country's total money supply to fall not merely by the same amount but rather in the same proportion as the fractional reserve of gold. Gold losses must have a magnified impact. To safeguard a 20 percent gold reserve, the authorities must allow or cause a $1 billion gold loss to shrink the money supply by $5 billion.

Many people who yearn for the good old days before World War I have an exaggerated idea of how long the international gold standard was in effect, of how automatically and smoothly it worked, and of how free from interference trade was in those days. Imports and exports kept in balance as well as they did because governments made preserving the gold redeemability of their currencies the overriding goal of financial policy. They had little scope to manage money supplies to suit themselves, even if full employment and price-level stability had been their objectives. Money supplies, prices, employment, production, and incomes had to respond to the requirements of keeping foreign transactions balanced at fixed exchange rates. Each country had to let deflation and inflation at home keep generally in step with world-wide monetary conditions. Capital movements providing temporary finance for imbalances were sometimes promoted by policies of raising interest rates in deficit countries and lowering them in surplus countries. In the longer run, these changes and the associated money-supply changes tended to lower or raise incomes and thereby contribute to adjustments in international trade.

A more nearly complete description of the historical gold standard and of how conditions were more favorable for it before World War I than they are nowadays would have to stress the world-wide dominance of a single financial center, London.

As far as any automatic trade-balancing processes at all are still at work under today's so-called gold-exchange standard (described in Chapter 7), they are diluted versions of the ones that worked before 1914. Before explaining this dilution, we shall describe a quite different system of international monetary relations, one both simpler to explain and simpler to operate.

FLEXIBLE EXCHANGE RATES

This simpler system stands at the opposite extreme from monetary linkage as tight as under the imaginary 100 percent international gold standard or as between Virginia and the other states. Yet this other system also avoids official settlement transactions in gold or foreign exchange. Each country has its own independent money, regulates its quantity to suit itself, and leaves its value free from a fixed tie to gold or to any foreign currency. Different currencies, therefore, exchange on the market in rough proportion to their purchasing powers over goods and services (see Chapter 6). Let us call the home currency the dollar and the currency of all other countries, lumped together, the crown. At the start, imports and exports (broadly defined) balance at an exchange rate of 4 crowns per dollar. Now something—inflation at home, depression abroad, a shift in preferences from home to foreign goods, or increased foreign competition with home exports—makes our imports exceed our exports. Import expenditures would exceed export earnings at the old exchange rate; dollars would be in excess supply and crowns in excess demand on the foreign-exchange market. Under this pressure, the dollar depreciates to 3 crowns, say; the crown appreciates to $33\frac{1}{3}$ cents. Translated into dollars at the new exchange rate, the prices of our imports and exports rise. This means a relative fall in our wages and in the prices of goods not important in international trade. Our people find import purchases less attractive and export sales more attractive than before. From the viewpoint of foreigners, lower prices in crowns of their imports and exports motivate increased purchases from and reduced sales to us. (Of course, these changes abroad are very slight if the rest of the world is very much larger than our country, so that the crown prices of actively traded goods are overwhelmingly determined on the world market and are little affected by the dollar's exchange rate. Loosely speaking, the smaller our country is in relation to the rest of the world, the more the price incentives to adjustment occur at home rather than abroad.)

Ideally, the *relative* prices of home and foreign goods and of slightly traded and actively traded goods undergo the same changes under the adjustment mechanism of the gold standard or similar fixed-exchange-rate system as under flexible exchange rates. But the smooth operation of the gold-standard mechanism is more dependent on an unrealistically high degree of downward as well as upward flexibility in domestic wages and prices. Curing a deficit under fixed exchange rates ideally requires the domestic general wage and price level to fall (unless, of course, opposite movements occur strongly enough abroad). Since this second of the above-listed processes will not shoulder the whole burden of adjustment, the unpleasant first process, involving employment and production levels, must operate. Under flexible exchange rates, by contrast, the relations between prices of home and foreign goods adjust through the exchange rate that makes them comparable; and the prices of import-and-export-type goods do most of the changing necessary for an appropriate relation between them and the prices of inactively traded goods and services. Under the exchange-rate mechanism, price changes in each national currency occur more selectively, where they are needed, in the foreign trade sector, and not through overall deflation or inflation. The gold-standard mechanism makes a wrong exchange rate right not by changing the rate itself but by adjusting everything else. This approach reminded Professor Wilhelm Röpke of a circus clown who, seeing that his chair was too far from the piano, struggled, with sweat streaming down his face, to push the piano toward the chair. Exchange-rate adjustment pushes the chair instead. It is a more delicate and selective method, operating directly where changes are really required—on the markets for internationally traded goods and services. Professor Milton Friedman has made a similar comparison. General price and income adjustments resemble arranging for more daylight time after work on summer evenings by having everyone adjust his daily schedule in detail so that he does everything one hour earlier. It is simpler to adopt daylight saving time. Changing the exchange rate instead of many internal prices offers similar simplicity. By being more selective and not working through total volumes of money and spending, the exchange-rate mechanism makes general contractions and expansions of employment, production, and incomes unnecessary for balance-of-payments adjustment. Each government can, if it wishes, insulate its country's money supply from external domination and try to stabilize its size or its growth rate as suits conditions at home.

The role of the exchange rate in balancing imports and exports helps explain why even countries with low average productivity can sell some of their goods cheaply enough to win markets abroad and why even countries with high average productivity can be undersold at home by foreigners on some goods. It also helps puncture the cheap-foreign-labor argument for tariffs and explains why no country, regardless of how high its wages and prices are, need be uncompetitive all across the board. With the exchange-rate mechanism allowed to operate, imports and exports (defined broadly, as suggested at the beginning of this chapter) do pay for each other. Their money prices do reflect real opportunity costs (assuming no serious domestic price distortions). The standard demonstration of the gains from trade applies, and businessmen do have price and profit incentives for the trade that reaps these gains. These same conclusions also hold when the trade-balancing mechanism of close monetary linkage is operating instead and domestic wages and prices are sufficiently flexible, though the stickiness of wages and prices in reality makes this other mechanism work less swiftly and surely.

A flexible exchange rate not only accomplishes necessary adjustments in a relatively efficient way but also helps avoid unnecessary ones. To understand how, we must distinguish between adjustments to real and to monetary disturbances. Inflation abroad would be an example of monetary disturbance. The resulting appreciation of the home currency in relation to the inflated foreign currency does not reduce the home-currency prices of import and export goods; it merely keeps them from rising as they would if the exchange rate were not allowed to reflect the foreign inflation. The flexible rate helps avoid the upward adjustment of the whole domestic price level and money supply that would be necessary under the fixed-rate mechanism to cure the balance-of-payments surplus caused by the foreign inflation. Conversely, depreciation of the home currency in response to foreign deflation does not unequivocally raise import and export prices but merely keeps them from falling as they otherwise would. Particularly in the case of deflation, however, the disturbance cannot be *purely* monetary. In practice, foreign countries could not experience deflation without also suffering depression and thus becoming less effectively eager trading partners for the home country than they had been. Thus, some "real" adjustment—some repatterning of resource allocation and of production and consumption—is necessary. But the adjustment is easier than if the home country had to adjust to foreign depression under fixed exchange rates. In fact, the adjustment even to a purely "real" disturbance is also easier under flexible than under fixed rates. When foreign demand for the home country's exports shrinks, the otherwise necessary fall in export prices or production is cushioned by exchange depreciation of the home currency. Depreciation avoids the *general* deflation of the home money supply and price level that would be necessary under the fixed-exchange-rate mechanism. (The appendix to this chapter examines the home money supply under fixed rates.)

POSSIBLE DIFFICULTIES
WITH THE EXCHANGE-RATE MECHANISM

Our condensed description oversimplifies automatic adjustment through flexible exchange rates, but it captures the essentials. The essential logic of alternative mechanisms is all that has concerned us so far; not until Chapters 9 and 10 do we survey all the advantages and disadvantages relevant to a policy choice among exchange-rate systems.

Right now, though, we must notice some possible complications in the working of flexible exchange rates. Some economists have worried that a currency's depreciation or devaluation (the distinction was explained on pages 13–14) could work perversely, worsening rather than curing a balance-of-payments deficit. This danger hinges on the possibility of very low price-sensitiveness of the home country's demand for imports and of the foreign demand for the home country's exports. An extreme case will make this clear: the physical quantities of imports and exports demanded do not change at all despite price changes. Contributing to the extreme character of this case, we also assume that foreigners will supply unlimited quantities of the home country's imports at an unchanged price in foreign currency and that the home country's export producers will supply unlimited quantities of their goods at an unchanged price in home currency. Now the authorities, hoping to cure a balance-of-payments deficit, devalue the home currency or let it depreciate. Translated at the new exchange rate, the home-currency price of imports has risen; but, by the assumptions just made, neither the quantity nor the total foreign-currency value of imports goes down. At the new exchange rate, both the price and total value of exports go down in foreign currency, since by assumption the foreigners buy no larger quantity than before. With the total foreign-currency value of imports unchanged and of exports reduced, the deficit has *worsened*.

For this perverse result, it is not necessary, after all, that the demands be absolutely insensitive to price. With the sensitivity slight enough (as specified by a formula not given here), the result would still be perverse. A freely fluctuating exchange rate would seem to be unworkable: a currency's free-market depreciation under pressure of a balance-of-payments deficit would worsen the deficit, lead to still further depreciation, and so on. But under such unlikely conditions, the price-level-adjustment mechanism of the gold standard would work just as perversely.

Actually, the price-sensitivity of demand for imports could not remain so disastrously low as the home currency depreciated. For as the home-currency price of imports rose, persistence in buying nearly unchanged physical quantities per time period would mean spending ever larger amounts of home money on them. People could not persist in doing so because they do not have unlimited incomes or unlimited holdings of money and other financial assets to spend out of. Because incomes and wealth are limited, the rise in the prices of foreign exchange and of imports would eventually force people to behave price-sensitively enough; further depreciation of the home currency would tend to shrink the deficit in the normal way after all. This is true, anyway, as long as continuous monetary inflation does not keep loosening the constraint of limited money incomes and money wealth. And if it did, inflation rather than low price-sensitivity of demand would be the straightforward explanation of why exchange-rate movements were not equilibrating the balance of payments.

A symmetrical argument applies to foreign buyers of the home country's exports. At some level of *appreciation* of the home currency (an extreme level opposite to the one just considered), the extremely high price of home exports in foreign currency would force foreign buyers to behave price-sensitively enough for the balance of payments to respond normally to the exchange rate.

Thus, even if there were a range of exchange rates in which the balance of payments responded perversely, that range would necessarily be flanked above and below by ranges of normal response; and there would have to be at least one stable-equilibrium exchange rate. Almost surely, though, the whole concept of perverse response is a mere theoretical toy. In reality, import and export demands are likely to be price-sensitive enough for normality in the vicinity of one single equilibrium exchange rate. Some factors promoting price-sensitivity include competition on the home market between imports and domestic substitutes and competition on the world market between the country's exports and similar goods supplied by other countries. The purchasing-power-parity doctrine, together with possibilities of arbitrage, explained in Chapter 6, also provides reassurance about a normal exchange-rate mechanism.

THE ABSORPTION APPROACH

We have just reviewed one strand of skepticism about adjustment through the exchange rate. Another is the "absorption approach." This analysis emphasizes that when a country is importing goods and services worth more in total than those it is exporting, it is *absorbing* goods and services—it is consuming and undertaking real investment —in excess of current national production. The country must be covering the excess absorption by disposing of gold, foreign exchange, or other previously acquired international assets, or by borrowing or receiving new investment funds or gifts from foreigners. Conversely, absorption falls short of current national production in a country running an export surplus on current account. Total absorption equals total production only when saving (that part of income produced but not consumed) just matches real investment (in buildings, machinery, inventories, and other capital goods).

The absorption approach considers the problem of a deficit in foreign trade by asking what currency devaluation or depreciation can do to reduce absorption relative to income, that is, to reduce investment relative to saving. Does it raise income without raising absorption as much or at all? Does it raise saving (reduce consumption) or reduce investment? Several effects are conceivable. Devaluation might somehow help put unemployed resources back into productive use or help obtain more output from resources already employed. It might raise prices and reduce the real value of cash balances, prodding individuals and businesses to reduce their consumption and investment in efforts to rebuild their real cash balances. It might somehow redistribute income from extravagant to thrifty people. But none of these or other "effects" mentioned in writings on the absorption approach seems strong and dependable.

To see how devaluation does, after all, raise the propensity to save or reduce the propensity to absorb out of income, we must realize that previously, in drawing down their external reserves to support the home currency on the foreign-exchange market, the authorities had been *subsidizing* absorption. They had been keeping import-and-export-type goods cheaper than otherwise in home money and in relation to home money incomes. They had been making the buying power of money incomes seem larger from the point of view of individual income-recipients than real income produced was from the national point of view. In the same way, the authorities had been keeping the total real buying power of domestic cash balances artificially high.

The deficit in trade implies overabsorption or undersaving by the country as a whole, *including* the rate-pegging agency. Yet private persons and businesses might have been living within their real incomes as they saw them. The country's deficit stemmed from a dissipation of the agency's resources and a related distortion of the prices that give meaning to money incomes and guide consumption and investment decisions. An end to exchange-rate pegging or a devaluation to an equilibrium level removes the price distortions that had been making real income seem larger from the viewpoints of ordinary persons and businesses than it was from the national viewpoint. This correction of price distortions is what, from the national point of view, reduces the propensity to spend or increases the propensity to save even out of a given real income. From their own points of view, however, individuals and businesses cut their absorption not because their propensities have changed but because their real incomes have declined.

The absorption approach paves the way for emphasizing the monetary nature of balance-of-payments deficits and difficulties. For an excess of absorption or expenditure over national income implies that individuals and businesses are running down their cash balances (and perhaps their other financial assets also, or running up their debts). Domestic money vanishes from circulation when it is paid into the central bank to buy foreign exchange at the pegged rate. The willingness of people to content themselves with shrunken cash balances in real terms and relative to income and expenditure spells a rise in velocity. A continuing balance-of-payments deficit thus depends on a continuing rise in velocity. Here, however, comes an important qualification. All this is true *unless* the monetary authority keeps on creating new domestic money to replace what it withdraws from circulation in selling foreign exchange. Whichever accompanies the balance-of-payments deficit—the implausible continuing rise in velocity or the continuing re-creation of domestic money—deserves emphasis as a monetary phenomenon.

In summary, each of the two approaches to understanding how exchange-rate changes work—the absorption approach and the approach emphasizing how demands respond to import and export prices—deals only implicitly with aspects of adjustment that the other stresses. The two can be reconciled by recognizing (1) how exchange rates affect the sizes of real incomes and real cash balances from the points of view of the persons who make decisions about consumption, saving, and investment and (2) how conditions affecting price-sensitivities of demand affect the scope and size of the subsidy to absorption that currency overvaluation affords and the size of the associated discrepancy between private and national views of real income. Reconciliation dispels the apparent pessimism of the absorption approach about the effectiveness of the exchange rate in equilibrating the balance of payments.

THE ADJUSTMENT OF TRADE
TO CAPITAL MOVEMENTS
UNDER FIXED EXCHANGE RATES

Capital movements and shifts in trade often occur in response to some common cause. Capital movements sometimes even adjust to trade. A rise in the foreign demand for a country's exports, for example, probably would give rise to an increased volume of short-term loans to foreigners in the form of sales to them on credit.

The opposite case of trade adjusting to an independently motivated capital movement has traditionally received more attention, however, for its explanation poses more of a challenge. Accepting the challenge will help confirm our understanding of balance-of-payments adjustment processes.

When a purely financial operation disturbs initial balance-of-payments equilibrium, how do "realities" accommodate themselves to it? What maintains or restores overall payments equilibrium? Suppose that Englishmen buy bonds issued by American companies (for realism, let us say in the nineteenth century). The American bond-issuers want dollars for buying labor and materials locally and have no particular demand for English goods. The English bond-buyers want an attractive yield on their savings and have no particular concern with export industries. If the bonds are denominated in dollars, the English lenders pay for the bonds after buying dollars with sterling. If the bonds are denominated in sterling, the American bond-issuers sell the sterling they receive for the dollars they really want. In either case, sterling is in excess supply and dollars are in excess demand on the market until the exchange rate changes.

Under the international gold standard, sterling moves toward its gold export point and the dollar toward its gold import point. Gold arbitrageurs come into action. The money supply, based on gold, shrinks in England and expands in the United States. Price levels and real incomes move with the money supplies, tending to promote English exports and American imports while restraining English imports and American exports. A net flow of real goods and services develops from England to the United States, matching the financial flow. England develops a surplus on current account matching its deficit on capital account during the period of the financial operations, and conversely for the United States.

Before mentioning some qualifications and refinements, let us note some basic points. A country receiving a net inflow of long-term capital will almost certainly receive net imports of goods and services (gold inflows or short-term capital outflows providing conceivable exceptions). This current-account deficit, far from being grounds for alarm, is the real counterpart of the financial flows. The rise of imports relative to exports of goods and services lets additional real resources become available in the borrowing country. To welcome an inflow of long-term capital while deploring a current-account deficit is to fight sheer arithmetic.

The real transfer of a capital movement need not take the form of capital goods. The borrowers may not want to buy any capital goods at all, or they may want ones that, like roads and buildings, cannot be imported and must be constructed locally. Perhaps imports of consumer goods will rise, freeing resources from producing similar goods locally and making them directly or indirectly available for the borrowers' projects. Resources might even become available through a fall in the borrowing country's exports. Since the borrowing country's import surplus need not take any particular form, the borrowing and lending countries can continue producing the kinds of goods in which they have comparative advantages.

It is not even necessary for the borrowing country to develop its current-account deficit and the lending country its current-account surplus in trade with each other. The borrowers and their fellow-countrymen may increase their spending not in the lending country but at home and in third countries; the lenders and their fellow-countrymen may reduce their spending not in the borrowing country but at home and in third countries. The third countries could keep their balances of payments in overall equilibrium while now running trade deficits with the lending country matched by trade surpluses with the borrowing country. This *multilateral* adjustment of trade to the capital movement would take place, if the gold-standard mechanism were working in ideal fashion, through a decline of prices in the lending country and a rise in the borrowing country, both relative to prices in third countries. The variety of countries as well as of goods and services that can take part in the international real transfer means that trade need not be distorted out of correspondence with comparative advantage, even though the financial side of the capital movement is arranged by borrowers and lenders in two countries only.

In the gold-standard case considered here, stabilizing speculation is likely to help hold exchange-rate movements within the gold points. As the exchange rate moves initially toward the gold export point of the lending country (the gold import point of the borrowing country), speculators may expect a rebound and buy lending-country currency while selling borrowing-country currency. In this way speculators move their short-term capital in the direction opposite to the primary long-term capital flow. So doing, they weaken the exchange-rate incentive for gold arbitrage and the impact it would have had on the two countries' money supplies. In a comparatively weak way, though, the speculators' actions still do tend to adjust trade to the primary capital movement. For the currency they buy comes out of the lending country's *active* money supply, while the previously idle currency they sell returns to the borrowing country's *active* money supply. (This statement oversimplifies a complicated process, but it hints at what happens.) Thus spending still tends to fall in the lending country and rise in the borrowing country, which helps (directly and through any price-level responses) to reduce absorption of resources in the one country and increase it in the other.

This aspect of the transfer process reminds us of a closely related one. The primary loan itself transfers purchasing power in a way appropriate to the real transfer. Because of the international loan, the lenders or their fellow-countrymen to whom they might otherwise have made loans do less spending than otherwise, while the borrowers or their fellow-countrymen whom they might otherwise have outbid for loans on the home capital market do more spending than otherwise. These effects probably help explain why trade often seemed to adjust itself with surprising speed to financial capital movements in the era of the historical gold standard and why actual gold and price-level movements seemed to play such a surprisingly small role in the process. If passive monetary and fiscal policies allowed the transfer of purchasing power and its direct effects on spending to touch off a downward spiral of employment, production, income, and expenditure in the lending country and an upward spiral in the borrowing country, these repercussions, too, would affect absorption of resources in the two countries in ways that helped adjust trade to the primary loan.

Under the present-day system of pegging exchange rates directly in a way that allows no scope for private gold arbitrage, capital movements nevertheless tend to affect national money supplies as they did under the historical gold standard; and the purchasing-power-transfer effects on trade are also similar. If domestic financial policies did not counteract these tendencies, the real side of international capital movements would develop nowadays much as it did under the gold standard.

THE ADJUSTMENT OF TRADE
TO CAPITAL MOVEMENTS
UNDER FLEXIBLE EXCHANGE RATES

With independent currencies and free exchange rates, the real transfer process would be rather different. When lending-country currency appears on the market in exchange for borrowing-country currency, nothing corresponding to gold arbitrage or official pegging holds exchange-rate movements within definite limits. Nor do the money supply and price level fall in the lending country and rise in the borrowing country. If anything (besides speculation) restrains exchange-rate movements, it is the response of trade itself to prices translated at the changed rates. The depreciation of the lending country's currency tends to reduce that country's imports and promote its exports in trade not only with the borrowing country but also with third countries, and the appreciation of the borrowing country's currency tends to promote that country's imports and reduce its exports in trade not only with the lending country but also with third countries. The adjustment of trade to the financial transfer is not restricted to bilateral channels or to any particular goods. Trade has at least as much scope for conforming to comparative advantage under free exchange rates as under the gold standard.

Although less probably than under the gold standard or the pegged-rate system, speculators might still buy the somewhat weakened currency of the lending country and sell previously held balances of the somewhat strengthened currency of the borrowing country. Any attendant withdrawal of money from active circulation in the lending country and return of money to active circulation in the borrowing country would join with the incentives of changed exchange rates in adjusting trade to the primary capital flow. Again as under the gold standard or pegged exchange rates, the very transfer of purchasing power away from the lenders (or from fellow-countrymen to whom they would otherwise have made loans) and to the borrowers (or to fellow-countrymen whom the borrowers would otherwise have outbid for loans) would also aid the adjustment. Because national money supplies are independent under free exchange rates, however, spending and income are more unlikely to spiral downward in the lending country and upward in the borrowing country than under fixed exchange rates. Instead, the exchange-rate movements themselves are the main element in adjusting trade to the capital movement.

If repayment of the loan eventually entails a net movement of capital from the debtor to the creditor country, the adjustment processes just described operate in the reverse direction.

THE DESTRUCTION OF ADJUSTMENT MECHANISMS

One reason for describing automatic trade adjustments in detail was to prepare for understanding how they might be blocked, and with what consequences. This insight is essential for understanding the present international monetary system. Problems of unbalanced trade and payments have plagued the world since the beginning of the Great Depression in 1929, and even earlier. They have been conspicuous since World War II. For several years after the war most countries other than the United States were beset with troubles collectively known as the "dollar shortage" (already mentioned in Chapter 4). Many a government was fixing the value of its own currency against the dollar at a higher level than would have prevailed in a free market. In countries where this was the policy, people found goods imported from the United States and a few other "hard-currency" countries a great bargain in local currency, while price incentives for export sales were weak. Even today the apparent need for controls to restrain overimporting plagues many countries, particularly in Asia and Latin America. Even Great Britain has experienced recurrent sterling crises causing worldwide anxiety. Besides devaluing the pound in 1949 and 1967, Britain has sometimes responded drastically both in trade policy and in domestic policy, as by imposing a 15 percent import duty surcharge in October 1964 and by attempting a certain amount of deflation at home in 1966.

In general, however, the 1950s brought great improvements, particularly in Europe. Postwar economic recoveries, slowdowns in inflation, a degree of informal coordination in domestic monetary policies, a few further exchange-rate adjustments following the widespread devaluations of 1949, continued heavy overseas spending by the United States government, and some lucky coincidences permitted relaxation of currency and trade restrictions. Balance-of-payments crises caused setbacks only ocasionally. At the end of 1958 the major West European countries restored external currency convertibility (defined on pages 15–16). As European troubles abated, significantly enough, American balance-of-payments troubles came to the fore.

It is hardly an oversimplification to blame the balance-of-payments troubles of the last few decades on the failure of governments to make up their minds about which set of automatic adjustment processes they will allow to operate. By and large, governments reject any monetary linkage as close as among the states of the United States nowadays or even as close as among countries before 1914. They dislike the threat of deflation of money supplies, prices, production, and employment transmitted through foreign trade. By the logic of the adjustment process compatible with the gold standard or other system of fixed exchange rates, domestic money supplies should shrink in countries with external deficits and expand in countries with external surpluses. At present, though, national monetary authorities generally counteract these spontaneous influences. Instead of letting national money supplies rise and fall as necessary for balance-of-payments equilibrium when conditions change, the authorities prefer to pursue domestic full-employment policies. Yet they will not untie their currencies and shun official dealings in gold and foreign exchange, for they fear the supposed horrors of fluctuating exchange rates. Instead, they indecisively look for a compromise between the two extremes of close monetary linkage and full monetary independence. The compromise consists largely of wishing and waiting for balance-of-payments difficulties somehow to go away of their own accord. Meanwhile, governments finance their exchange-rate pegging by drawing down (or, in times of surplus, building up) their gold and foreign-exchange reserves. Official borrowing from the International Monetary Fund (see Chapter 7) and from foreign central banks ekes out skimpy reserves. In cases of stubborn imbalance, governments sometimes slightly modify their domestic money-supply, interest-rate, and tax-and-spending policies in the direction the gold standard would have required. Occasionally, they even adjust exchange rates. This remedy has become unpopular, however, because of unhappy experiences with speculation when adjustments were in preparation or even were being falsely rumored.

Finally, today's compromise system, lacking the automatic adjustment properties of either extreme system—permanently fixed or completely free exchange rates—sometimes breeds tariff increases, tightening of import quotas, restrictions on lending and investing abroad, and requisitioning of foreign exchange earned and rationing of foreign exchange to be spent.

Theory and experience have time and again shown that three things are not permanently compatible: (1) fixed exchange rates, (2) independent national monetary policies, and (3) continuous freedom of trade from controls to force a balance in international transactions. Before World War I, countries generally sacrificed the second of these. (One suggested reason is that wages and prices were more flexible downwards in those days than now, so that they could absorb more of the impact and let employment and production and real incomes absorb less of the impact of shrinkage in money supplies and spending in deficit countries. In those days, furthermore, the very idea of monetary-fiscal policy for full employment had not yet caught hold.) Nowadays, in the spirit of indecisive compromise, countries generally sacrifice each of the three desirable conditions in some degree. Countries have not yet made a clear-cut choice between fixed exchange rates and monetary independence. Their incompatibility is a great obstacle to liberal trade policies.

REFERENCES

1. FRITZ MACHLUP. "Adjustment, Compensatory Correction, and Financing of Imbalances in International Payments." In Robert E. Baldwin and others, *Trade, Growth, and the Balance of Payments* (essays in honor of Gottfried Haberler); Chicago: Rand McNally & Company, 1965, pp. 185–213.

2. J. E. MEADE. *The Balance of Payments*. London: Oxford University Press, 1951. Especially chapters XI through XV.

3. GOTTFRIED HABERLER. *Prosperity and Depression,* 4th ed.; London: Allen & Unwin, 1958. Chapter 12.

4. EGON SOHMEN. *Flexible Exchange Rates, Theory and Controversy*. Chicago: University of Chicago Press, 1961.

5. FRITZ MACHLUP. *International Payments, Debts, and Gold*. New York: Charles Scribner's Sons, 1964. Essays II, VIII, and XV through XX.

APPENDIX: EXCHANGE-RATE PEGGING AND THE DOMESTIC MONEY SUPPLY

The balance-of-payments adjustment mechanism appropriate to a gold standard or other fixed-rate system depends on a link between changes in countries' gold or foreign-exchange reserves and in their home money supplies. As we now examine this link in more detail, we should not let the existence of two distinct types of "reserves" confuse us—the external or gold-and-foreign-exchange reserves of the central bank or similar monetary authority and the domestic reserves that commercial banks hold against their deposits.

MONETARY CHANGES
AND THEIR NEUTRALIZATION

When the central bank of a country with a payments deficit sells foreign exchange to support its currency, it shrinks the supply of domestic central-bank deposits and currency that serve as reserves for the commercial banks. This domestic "high-powered" money shrinks much the same as if the central bank had been selling government securities on the open market. The commercial banks can continue making net sales of foreign exchange to their customers only because they are in turn buying foreign exchange from the central bank on the interbank wholesale market. They pay for it from the domestic reserve balances they hold at the central bank. Under a fractional-reserve system and with bank loans and investments and deposits initially expanded fully to the limit permitted by their reserves, the commercial banks must contract their customers' deposits by several times as much as the system's losses of "high-powered" reserve money. The contraction would be inadequate if the banks merely failed to re-create the deposits drawn down by their customers in payment for net purchases of foreign exchange.

In selling foreign exchange, the central bank is financing the country's balance-of-payments deficit. It is also both thwarting yet promoting adjustment. Keeping the exchange rate pegged thwarts the exchange-rate mechanism, but shrinking domestic bank reserves promotes a deflationary adjustment of the gold-standard type. The multiple contraction of domestic bank-account money restrains spending, including spending on imports and on exportable goods.

To avoid causing a business recession, the central bank may act to offset the contractionary effect of its foreign-exchange sales; it may buy domestic securities to restore domestic reserve funds to the commercial banks. Professor Fritz Machlup calls this antideflationary action the "domestic financing" of the country's balance-of-payments deficit. He distinguishes it from the "external financing" represented by the central bank's sale of foreign exchange. The distinction is crucial. While the domestic money-supply shrinkage due to the external financing tends to promote balance-of-payments adjustment, the domestic financing that offsets this shrinkage thwarts adjustment.

The policy of re-expanding domestic money and credit returns to domestic spenders the domestic money collected for the foreign exchange sold. It lets spending continue on imported and exportable as well as on domestic goods. Neither the exchange-rate mechanism nor anything resembling the gold-standard mechanism then operates to correct the external deficit. Domestic offsetting is usual enough to justify the generalization that no automatic balance-of-payments adjustment mechanism is allowed to operate in the present-day world.

Much the same holds true in reverse for a country with a payments surplus. When buying foreign exchange to keep the home currency from appreciating beyond its upper support limit, the central bank pays with newly created deposits of its own, supplying the commercial banks with "high-powered" domestic reserves and setting the stage for multiple expansion of ordinary bank-deposit money. This domestic monetary impact is much the same as if the central bank had been buying government securities on the open market. The resulting rise in spending and domestic prices would tend to spur imports, restrain exports, and eliminate the balance-of-payments surplus in the gold-standard way. To resist inflation, however, the central bank might neutralize these domestic monetary repercussions by selling securities on the open market. Alternatively, the central bank, cooperating with the government, might refrain in the first place from creating new "high-powered" money to pay for its net purchases of foreign exchange. Instead, it might pay with funds withdrawn from the public by a government budget surplus. The automatic correction of the balance-of-payments surplus would still be lost.

RESISTING IMPORTED INFLATION

As European experience in the 1950s and early 1960s illustrated, it is inconvenient fully to resist the inflationary pressures of a strong balance-of-payments surplus. A domestic tight-money policy designed to offset the expansionary influence of the central bank's purchases of foreign exchange is likely to attract funds from abroad seeking high interest yields. Domestic business firms and banks, squeezed for funds, may seek loans abroad. If capital movements are substantially free of controls and if confidence in the fixed exchange rates is firm, a commercial bank in need of domestic reserve funds can in effect obtain them on the international money market: funds borrowed abroad can be sold at the fixed exchange rate for newly created domestic reserve balances at the central bank. Blocking this escape from domestic monetary policy requires ambitious control or manipulation of the foreign assets and liabilities of domestic commercial banks. Ironically enough, international capital movements are likely to prove troublesome whether confidence or distrust in the fixed exchange rates prevails: confidence gives scope for interest-sensitive capital movements; distrust breeds speculation.

Successful resistance to inflation imported through a balance-of-payments surplus, even if technically possible, has real costs. Foreign-exchange reserves accumulated by the central bank bear relatively low rates of interest and are hardly attractive investments in their own right, as indicated by the fact that private parties leave such investments to the central bank instead of undertaking them all themselves. Tightening monetary or fiscal policy to offset the inflationary impact of the central bank's purchases of foreign exchange means squeezing domestic borrowers or taxpayers for the sake of the cheap loans to foreigners that the foreign-exchange acquisitions represent. Another cost is the additional complexity imposed on framing and implementing domestic monetary-fiscal policy when the authorities must try to predict and allow for balance-of-payments developments and sometimes try to offset their domestic impacts. The authorities may still succeed in resisting imported inflation if they give price stability high enough priority and are willing to incure the costs connected with letting the balance-of-payments surplus persist uncorrected, but they are unlikely to succeed unless they understand the complications and costs involved.

SOME INSTITUTIONAL POINTS

So far we have assumed that the central bank is the agency engaged in both pegging exchange rates and managing domestic bank reserves and, through them, the money supply. As an administrative arrangement for neutralizing the domestic monetary impacts of foreign-exchange operations more nearly automatically, some countries have a separate exchange fund or office. The British Exchange Equalization

Account is an example. It holds an inventory of domestic Treasury bills as well as of gold and foreign exchange. When it sells foreign exchange, it ordinarily returns the domestic funds taken in payment to the domestic money market by investing them in Treasury bills. (It might as well buy bills on the open market, for when it acquires "tap" bills from the Treasury, it spares the Treasury that much financing on the market.) When the Account buys foreign exchange, it pays with domestic funds obtained not by creating them but by selling Treasury bills from its portfolio. (It might as well sell the bills on the open market, for when it obtains domestic funds by redeeming "tap" bills at the Treasury, it forces the Treasury to finance itself by issuing more bills on the market.) Such an agency joins together, administratively, exchange-rate-stabilization operations and operations that offset their domestic monetary impacts semiautomatically. Earlier, we described the two parts of the combined operations separately to focus attention on the part promoting and the part resisting balance-of-payments adjustment and also to clarify the domestic problem requiring some treatment or other. Typically, the exchange fund or office is not a completely separate agency but is managed by the central bank. Especially in theoretical discussions not concerned with administrative details of particular countries, it is convenient to blanket all of a country's agencies concerned with external and domestic monetary policy together under the label of "the monetary authorities."

So far we have been referring to an advanced country with a well-developed financial system, a profit-oriented fractional-reserve banking system, and a money supply consisting more of bank deposits than of currency. In a less developed country, gains and losses of foreign-exchange reserves are likely to have less scope for touching off *multiple* expansions and contractions of the domestic money supply. On the other hand, domestic monetary policy is less likely to neutralize a comparatively close and automatic gearing of the money supply to the balance of payments. In a number of smaller countries, the money supply consists either of foreign currency or of domestic issues backed by foreign exchange. The only real difference is that issuing domestic money backed by foreign exchange lets the local government earn some interest on its reserves.

Some technicalities of how the domestic money supply responds to the balance of payments are different in the United States than elsewhere. The American authorities intervene directly on the foreign-exchange market only to a minor extent. For the most part they just stand ready to buy gold from and sell gold to foreign authorities at a fixed dollar price. Many foreign authorities hold dollar deposits at the Federal Reserve Bank of New York as minor parts of their external reserves. These foreign-owned funds are not part of the reserve base of the American commercial banking system. But when a foreign central bank sells some of these dollars to support its own currency, they come into the possession of ordinary merchants and financiers who spend or invest them in the United States, where they are deposited in commercial banks. They thus enter into the heart of the American financial system: Federal Reserve funds formerly under foreign ownership come into the possession of commercial banks as additions to their reserves of "high-powered dollars." Conversely, when a foreign central bank buys dollars and transfers them to its account at the Federal Reserve Bank of New York (perhaps at a time of United States balance-of-payments deficit), it withdraws them from the reserves of the United States commercial banking system and exerts a contractionary influence on the United States money supply. Of course, the Federal Reserve is likely to offset this influence by open-market operations.

In practice, foreign authorities generally hold only small working balances at the Federal Reserve. They keep more of their dollar reserves on deposit at United States commercial banks or in Treasury bills and other short-term investments. By acquiring dollars in those forms, they do not drain domestic reserves away from American banks. The drain occurs when a foreign authority converts some of its dollars into gold. It buys gold from the United States Treasury, paying by check on its deposit at the Federal Reserve Bank of New York, which it had built up either by transferring funds previously on deposit at a commercial bank or by selling money-market instruments from its portfolio. The payment by the foreign authority builds up the Treasury's balance at the Federal Reserve Bank, but the Treasury promptly draws that balance down again to retire and cancel the gold certificates it had previously deposited in the Federal Reserve Bank when it issued them upon acquiring the gold now sold. In the whole set of operations, the key influence on the United States money supply is the loss of domestic reserve funds by the commercial banks: the banks lose Federal Reserve funds when the foreign authority transfers to the Federal Reserve deposits previously held with them or when, alternatively, they honor checks drawn by their depositors in payment for money-market instruments bought from the foreign authority.

A Treasury purchase of gold imported from abroad (or mined in the United States) tends, conversely, to expand the reserves of the commercial banks. The Treasury pays by check on its account at the Federal Reserve, which it replenishes by depositing gold certificates it issues against the newly acquired gold. When the seller of the gold deposits his Treasury check in a commercial bank, the banking system acquires Federal Reserve funds.

Though it is not usual, direct "sterilization" can keep gold transactions from having a net effect on domestic bank reserves. From late 1936 until early 1938, for example, the United States Treasury "sterilized" gold bought from abroad. Instead of creating gold certificates to replenish its Federal Reserve balances drawn down in payment, it sold Treasury bills. The whole operation amounted to buying gold and offsetting its usual domestic expansionary effect by an open-market sale of securities, except that the expansionary and offsetting operations were telescoped together and that the Treasury rather than the Federal Reserve undertook the open-market sale of securities.

Conversely, a gold sale would not be contractionary if the Treasury offset the foreign authority's withdrawal of deposits from the commercial banks or sale of money-market investments by itself buying government securities in the open market (or by letting some of its obligations mature without issuing new ones). The Treasury could pay for these securities with Federal Reserve funds received from the foreign gold-buyer, and it could avoid retiring gold certificates if it had previously been holding enough "sterilized" gold.

Not all imbalances of payments change the United States money supply. When a United States deficit is "settled" by foreign acquisition of ordinary domestic bank balances and securities, the banking system loses no reserve funds. Only the ownership of bank balances or securities changes then, especially if private foreigners acquire deposits in United States commercial banks to use them as working balances much as Americans do. Since deficits settled this way do not shrink the United States money supply, they have no strong tendency to be self-correcting. The opportunity to settle much of its external deficit in its own money is the privilege of a key-currency country, a country whose currency enjoys wide international use as working balances and as official reserves. It is a feature much emphasized by some critics of today's so-called gold-exchange standard (described more fully in Chapter 7).

SUMMARY

Two points deserve re-emphasis. The automatic link between a country's balance of payments and its domestic money supply works in connection with official exchange-rate-stabilizing transactions or gold transactions. If such stabilization were discontinued, along with related transactions such as switches of funds owned by foreign authorities between commercial-bank deposits or money-market instruments and deposits at the central bank, the gold-standard-type automatic tendencies toward external adjustment would give way to the mechanism of flexible exchange rates. Secondly, much can be done—and usually is done—even under fixed exchange rates to neutralize the domestic monetary impact of imbalances of payments. Still, a country's exposure to deflationary and inflationary impacts operating through the balance of payments complicates the tasks of policy-makers, especially since the neutralization that may seem advisable on domestic grounds largely destroys any automatic external balancing mechanism.

REFERENCES

1. Fritz Machlup. "Adjustment, Compensatory Correction, and Financing of Imbalances in International Payments." In Robert E. Baldwin and others, *Trade, Growth, and the Balance of Payments* (essays in honor of Gottfried Haberler); Chicago: Rand McNally & Company, 1965, pp. 185–213.

2. Richard Ward. *International Finance.* Englewood Cliffs, N. J.: Prentice-Hall, Inc., 1965. Chapter 9.

EQUILIBRIUM OF SPOT

AND FORWARD EXCHANGE

RATES

PURCHASING-POWER PARITY

Supply and demand determine a freely flexible exchange rate. A fixed exchange rate can work satisfactorily if domestic policies influence supplies and demands so as to make them balance tolerably well at the chosen rate.

The purchasing-power-parity doctrine concerns the level at which supply and demand will balance. The doctrine notes that people value currencies for what they will buy. If one American dollar buys as much goods and services as three foreign crowns, a free exchange rate would hover in the range of three crowns per dollar, 33 cents per crown. An actual rate that unmistakably undervalued the crown, say 25 cents, would make foreign goods seem great bargains to Americans and make American goods seem overpriced to foreigners. American eagerness to buy foreign goods and foreign reluctance to buy American goods would flood the foreign-exchange market with dollars seeking to buy scarce crowns. The imbalance would bid the rate back toward its purchasing-power parity. Corrective pressures would operate through changes in both the quantities and the mix of goods traded. Undervaluation of the crown would make the general price level of foreign productive factors relatively low in dollars, enabling foreign businessmen to compete in the American market with an expanded variety of goods, while restricting foreign purchases in variety as well as in volume. Responses of trade that might be small in relation to total imports and exports could still be large in relation to any initial balance-of-payments surplus or deficit.

A comparison of two countries' price levels to compute a purchasing-power parity presupposes some one assortment of goods and services that can be priced in both countries and that accurately represents the types and relative quantities of various goods and services produced and consumed in each. In fact, though, no one assortment can typify the patterns of production and consumption in both of two countries. A direct comparison of the purchasing powers of two currencies is thus impractical, as explained more fully below. A makeshift is necessary: the current parity rate is estimated from *changes* in the purchasing powers of the two currencies since some past base period when the actual exchange rate was supposedly in equilibrium. If the American price level has tripled over a certain period of time while the foreign level has been multiplied by six—if foreigners have suffered twice as much price inflation as Americans —then the dollar should be worth about twice as many crowns as before. The convenience of using each country's own price index, constructed in its own way and representative of the local economy, is also a source of weakness. The purchasing-power-parity doctrine is mainly concerned with the forces at work determining an exchange rate at a given time; what may have happened in the past is ancient history. Yet the makeshift calculations deal with price-level changes over a span of time, during which many sorts of changes may have robbed price indexes of accuracy and even of clear meaning. For many reasons, moreover, the base-period actual exchange rate used in the calculation may not have been an equilibrium rate. Tariffs and other trade barriers may have become more or less severe since the base period.

STABILIZING PRESSURES

All these difficulties concern makeshift parity calculations; they do not impugn the logic of the purchasing-power-parity doctrine itself. Fundamentally, the doctrine describes stabilizing pressures that keep an exchange rate from oscillating chaotically and that keep pushing the rate toward a definite equilibrium level, hard though it may be to specify a precise figure. The fact that even makeshift parity calculations generally correspond reasonably well with actual exchange rates helps dispel the worry that a free exchange rate might be unstable because of extremely low price-sensitivities of demand. So far as the parity doctrine holds true, supply and demand in international trade respond sensitively enough to prices not to require extreme divergent shifts in the prices of domestic and international goods to correct balance-of-payments disequilibriums. Furthermore, so far as approximate equilibrium is maintained continuously, shifts from disequilibrium to equilibrium are not observed, and neither are conspicuous shifts in the relative price levels of internationally traded and domestic goods.

The well-known standard objections to the purchasing-power-parity doctrine are not really conclusive. As for the transportation costs that may keep an exchange rate between two currencies from corresponding to their relative purchasing powers, these costs merely keep the rate from adhering closely to purchasing-power parity but do not discredit the concept of parity itself. Similarly, the costs of shipping gold keep an exchange rate under the international gold standard from staying exactly at mint par without discrediting that concept. In permitting deviations from exact parity, transportation costs of gold under the international gold standard and of goods and services under independent paper currencies differ in degree but not in kind.

Many transactions besides those in goods and services admittedly give rise to supply and demand on the foreign-exchange market, yet they can push free exchange rates out of line with relative price levels only within limits. These limits, imprecise though they may be, are essentially what the parity doctrine is all about. Just as gold arbitrage limits deviations of gold-standard exchange rates from their mint pars, even though transactions in many things besides gold give rise to supply of and demand for currencies, so arbitrage in goods and services can limit deviations of free exchange rates from purchasing-power parities. If nontrade transactions were tending to drive a free exchange rate markedly away from purchasing-power parity, the resulting price incentives would affect imports and exports so as to hold the discrepancy in check. Just as gold-standard exchanges fluctuate within the gold points, so paper exchanges fluctuate within "commodity points" that depend on the costs of and other obstacles to shipping commodities. Actually, an exchange rate has not just a single pair of upper and lower commodity points but many—one pair for each good or service actually or potentially entering into international trade. Strictly speaking, an exchange rate has just as many purchasing-power pars: for each commodity or service marketed in both of two countries, there is some potential level of the exchange rate that would equate the two local-currency prices. *The* purchasing-power parity is some sort of central tendency among these individual parities. As an actual exchange rate departs further and further from this average parity, it passes the import or export points of more and more individual commodities; and what amounts to arbitrage in these commodities provides a "defense in depth" against further movement of the rate.

The theories of mint par under the gold standard and of purchasing-power parity are both theories of par. Neither insists that exchange rates stay precisely at par and stands or falls according to whether or not they do. Both theories describe correctives—arbitrage in gold in the one case, in tradable goods and services in the other—that restrain wide departures from par. This point is the answer, incidentally, to the further objection that not only prices but also income levels influence trade and exchange rates. Changes in technology and tastes also affect exchange rates. However, the purchasing-power-parity doctrine still describes price-induced adjustments in flows of trade that will limit nonmonetary exchange-rate movements, especially for countries not narrowly specialized in producing only a few commodities. Although "real" changes can, within limits, modify a systematic distortion of an exchange rate from some calculated parity, the rate can still be highly stable in the sense that price incentives will limit or reverse, rather than intensify, random departures.

Tariffs, quotas, exchange controls, and other man-made trade barriers, if restrictive enough, could ruin the responsiveness of trade to prices and so make the parity doctrine irrelevant. The doctrine is meant to deal with relatively free markets and, in fact, to help appraise their workability. Rigorous controls may make the doctrine, like many other propositions of economic theory, an incomplete description of what really happens.

BIAS DUE TO INCOME DIFFERENTIALS

One more difficulty, in addition to those already mentioned, raises doubt whether the equilibrium exchange rate between two currencies is the simple ratio of their purchasing powers. Yet it does not discredit the more fundamental concept of a stable equilibrium rate systematically and closely *related* to their purchasing powers.

To compare the purchasing powers of the dollar and the crown (which we now suppose to be the currency of a relatively poor European country), we want to price the same "basket" of goods and services in dollars in the United States and in crowns in Europe. But which country's consumption or production pattern shall determine the make-up of the basket? Each country's basket may be unrepresentative of economic life in the other country, and a compromise basket may be unrepresentative of both.

Another way to see the problem is to ask where the cost of living is lower. The answer depends on which country's consumption pattern is used in the comparison. At the pattern of exchange rates that would balance each country's overall payments, the cost of American-style living is likely to be lower in the United States than in Europe. The reason is that certain goods and services figure more heavily in the American than in the European consumption pattern precisely because they *are* cheaper in relation to other goods in the United States than in Europe. At the same time and at the same equilibrium rates, the cost of a European assortment of goods is likely to be higher in the United States. The reason is that some things carry more weight in the European than the American consumption pattern because they are less expensive in relation to other things in Europe than in the United States. In short, the purchasing power of each currency seems greater when its own country's basket of goods, rather than the other's, is used in the comparison. An extreme example will make this clear: If the American basket contains some good or service completely unobtainable in Europe, its price in crowns in Europe will be infinitely high, while its price in dollars in the United States will be some definite figure only.

How is all this relevant? The commodity-arbitrage strand of purchasing-power-parity reasoning applies only to goods that do or could enter into international trade. But if the price-level comparison is made with a basket including some goods that are especially high-priced in the United States but are absent from or unimportant in international trade, the comparison will make the dollar's purchasing-power parity seem weaker than its trade-balancing equilibrium rate on the crown.

A country's relatively high per capita income level may cause an underestimate of its currency's equilibrium value in this way. The reason is that in a rich country, nontradable goods—services, typically—tend to be relatively high priced and to make the country's *general* price level too high in relation to the narrower price level of the tradable goods that can enter into commodity arbitrage.

But *why* are nontradable services more expensive relative to tradable goods in rich than in poor countries? A country is likely to be rich precisely because its labor and other factors of production are used more productively than those of a poor country. But its advantage in productivity is not uniform all across the board. It is greater in tradable goods, smaller in services. The reason is that technological advances in production are more likely to affect tradable goods of farm and factory than nontradable services. High-labor-content goods like custom-made articles and buildings also tend to lag behind in technical advance. Since labor of similar qualifications tends to receive the same wage in all equally attractive occupations, high-labor-content services and nontraded goods tend to be high-priced relative to traded goods in high-productivity rich countries and low-priced relative to traded goods in low-productivity poor countries. Residents of rich countries traveling abroad commonly notice this: as translated at trade-balancing exchange rates (in determining which the prices of traded goods are particularly relevant), prices in poor countries seem quite low for domestic help, haircuts, and other services.

Saying that only the prices of traded goods are *directly* relevant to the equilibrium exchange rate might seem to reduce the purchasing-

power-parity doctrine to an uninteresting truism, since, at a given
exchange rate, trade would make internationally traded goods have
the same prices everywhere by raising the prices of particular goods
in countries exporting them and lowering their prices in countries
importing them. What saves the doctrine from sterility is the fact that,
far from determining the levels at which the prices of tradable goods
are equal at home and abroad, a free exchange rate is much more
nearly the *result* of this equalization tendency. Furthermore, although the prices of tradable goods tend to be the same in different
countries (apart from transportation costs and the like), the prices of
tradable and nontradable goods are linked within each country. The
links operate through costs of production and values in use—for
example, through the competition among different lines of production
for the same labor and ingredients and through substitutabilities for
consumers among different goods and services. These links justify
going beyond truistically comparing the price levels of traded goods
only and comparing general price levels instead.

Even though the prices of traded and nontraded goods and services
are linked together within rich and poor countries alike, they are
linked in different patterns of relative prices. The purchasing powers
of rich countries' currencies are relatively higher in buying traded
goods than in buying goods and services in general, including nontraded ones. Yet the narrower purchasing powers over traded goods
are the ones directly relevant to equilibrium exchange rates. Thus,
purchasing-power parities calculated with general price levels seem to
call for weaker exchange rates for the currencies of rich countries
than the rates that would in fact yield balance-of-payments equilibrium.

Bela Balassa tested this proposition by studying how the ratios of
purchasing-power-parity to actual exchange rates were associated with
per capita gross national products for a number of countries. Accepting actual exchange rates as approximations of equilibrium rates, he
found that the higher a country's per capita gross national product,
the weaker, by and large, was its calculated parity exchange rate
relative to its actual rate. This relation between a country's productivity and per capita income, on the one hand, and the ratio of the
general-price-level calculation of its parity exchange rate to the rate
that would yield balance-of-payments equilibrium, on the other hand,
may, if it proves fairly dependable, serve as a way of correcting the

crude parity calculation in estimating whether an existing exchange rate undervalues or overvalues a particular currency.

In case the bias in question is still not quite clear, a look at it from another angle may be helpful. Translating the money incomes of different countries at the exchange rates that yield balance-of-payments equilibrium tends to exaggerate the real-income differential between rich and poor countries. The reason is that nontraded goods and services tend to be relatively cheap in poor countries. This circumstance does not directly affect the actual or equilibrium exchange rates used in comparing money incomes, but it does affect the domestic purchasing powers of money incomes. The cheapness of services, though having little direct influence on equilibrium exchange rates, means that the purchasing powers of money incomes in poor countries are larger than their translation at equilibrium exchange rates suggests. The exchange rates appropriate for payments equilibrium are weaker for poor countries' currencies and stronger for rich countries' currencies than the rates appropriate for international real-income comparisons.

In describing the bias toward underestimating both the domestically relevant purchasing power of a poor country's currency and the internationally relevant purchasing power of a rich country's currency, we have been taking for granted a direct comparison of the total prices of standard assortments of goods and services at a given point in time. Does the same bias affect what we have called the "makeshift" comparisons of *changes* in the purchasing powers of currencies since some base period? Will the relative purchasing power of a rich country's currency appear to have risen too little or sunk too much, so that the comparison of index numbers, like the direct price-level comparison, would misrepresent the equilibrium exchange rate as an overvaluation of the rich country's currency? Yes, the bias would operate if, over time, the extent had widened to which the rich country enjoyed a greater productivity advantage in traded goods than in nontraded services. This may well be a realistic case because of the tendency of technical progress to continue occurring especially on the farms and in the factories of advanced countries. If this sectoral unevenness of productivity advantage had not increased, however, a comparison of purchasing-power *changes* would sidestep the bias in question.

IMPERFECT CALCULATIONS
BUT NOT RANDOM RATES

The existence of this bias, especially if it turns out to defy accurate assessment, again emphasizes that the purchasing-power-parity doctrine is not fundamentally a guide to actually setting equilibrium exchange rates. Fundamentally, the doctrine argues that an equilibrium rate between each two currencies tends to emerge from market forces and that random deviations from it tend to be strongly self-correcting, even though actually calculating that precise rate in advance and then imposing it, as distinguished from just observing what happens on the market, may hardly be possible. In short, the stabilizing-pressures aspect of the doctrine is more fundamental than the rate-calculation aspect. The fairly good general correspondence of calculated parities and actual exchange rates that we can find despite all the biases and inaccuracies that might interfere strengthens our confidence in the stabilizing pressures that the doctrine describes. Biases and other problems of actual calculation further explain why the discrepancies observed between calculated parities and actual exchange rates (small discrepancies, usually) do not show any haphazard determination of actual rates. Those discrepancies largely reflect systematic correspondence with objective economic conditions.

EXCHANGE RISK AND FORWARD EXCHANGE

An exchange rate may change to a businessman's disadvantage between his negotiating and his completing an international transaction. Suppose an American importer orders English goods and agrees to pay for them in pounds sterling three months later. If the dollar price of sterling rises in the interval, he loses. Of course, he would gain from a fall in the rate on sterling; the *risk* is the problem. The risk is obvious under freely fluctuating exchange rates. Even under pegged rates, there is some risk of loss from fluctuations within the support limits, as well as the risk of official rate adjustments. The importer can avoid the risk (and give up his chance of gain) by making a *forward-exchange contract* with his bank at the very time he agrees to buy the English goods. The contract specifies the exchange rate, known as the *forward exchange rate,* at which he will buy and the bank will sell a definite number of pounds sterling at an exactly or approximately specified future date. *Forward exchange* itself is foreign exchange bought and sold in this way—for future delivery.

Is the bank gambling on future exchange-rate movements when it makes such contracts? No; it will be making them in both directions. It will be agreeing to sell foreign exchange in the future to some customers and to buy it from others. Of course, an individual bank's forward sales to and purchases from its own customers are unlikely to match exactly. But different banks can cancel out their imbalances among each other. A bank overcommitted to sell a certain currency in the future will quickly arrange to buy it from another bank whose overcommitments happen to run in the opposite direction. A "wholesale" market for interbank trading in forward and spot exchange alike operates over the telephone in major financial centers. (*Spot exchange* is ordinary foreign exchange, traded for delivery immediately or within a couple of days.) Telephone and teletype facilities link the interbank markets in different countries.

We have just seen the main reason why it is wrong to say that forward exchange contracts provide insurance against the risks of exchange-rate changes. Insurance spreads the losses from essentially unavoidable risks around in sure but small pieces known as insurance premiums. Forward-exchange transactions, instead of pooling or sharing risks in this way, *destroy* risk by cancelling opposite risks out against each other. Traders who use forward-exchange contracts are *not* paying insurance premiums to spread exchange-rate risk around. They are not dealing at forward exchange rates systematically less favorable to themselves than the spot rates would have been. They are not paying any such risk premiums, premiums that they would supposedly have to shift partly to producers of internationally traded goods in the form of lower prices and to consumers in the form of higher prices than would prevail if exchange rates were rigidly and permanently fixed. (This is not to say that forward-exchange contracts can eliminate every vestige of risk connected with exchange rates. The qualifications that would be appropriate here, however, are too minor to be worth the necessary space. The residual risks are almost certainly smaller than those of other kinds that would be imposed by the policies necessary to keep exchange rates permanently fixed.)

INTEREST PARITY

An alert reader will not yet be convinced. He will wonder what makes purchases and sales of forward exchange just match each other at forward rates reasonably close to spot rates. Might not big premiums or discounts of forward from spot rates be necessary to clear the market?

The answer is that *covered interest arbitrage* tends to fill any gaps between forward supply and demand stemming from ordinary transactions, and fill the gaps at forward rates that *are* closely related to spot rates. As mentioned in Chapter 2, arbitrage consists of transactions undertaken to profit from price discrepancies between markets. Covered interest arbitrage consists of transactions to profit from departures from a certain relation between spot and forward exchange rates and interest rates in different countries. A couple of examples will help explain this relation, known as *interest parity*. Suppose—just to understand why so big a discrepancy could not last—that sterling for delivery in three months commands a 10 percent higher price in dollars than spot sterling does. At the same time, interest rates are the same in London and New York. Arbitrageurs can now profit by buying sterling spot and simultaneously selling it three-months forward. During the three months they put their sterling on loan in London. For the arbitrage to be unprofitable, the interest rate on sterling would have to be approximately 10 percentage points per three months (40 points a year) lower in London than the interest rate paid on dollars borrowed (or forgone on dollars owned) in New York. With the two interest rates equal, as assumed, the strong pressure of arbitrageurs' spot purchases and forward sales of sterling tends to raise the spot and lower the forward rate on sterling and eliminate or shrink the discrepancy between them.

For another example, suppose that the relevant interest rate is one percentage point per three months (four points a year) higher in London than in New York. If forward and spot exchange rates happened to be the same, arbitrageurs could profitably borrow in New York, buy spot sterling, relend at the higher London interest rate, and transfer their funds back into dollars at the end of three months under forward contracts made at the beginning of the whole operation. The pressure of arbitrageurs' spot purchases and forward sales of sterling would push the dollar price of three-months forward sterling to a discount of approximately one percent from the spot price, a discount corresponding to the interest-rate differential. (In principle, although probably only slightly, even the interest rates in the two countries in both our examples would take part in the mutual adjustment of all the variables to an equilibrium pattern.)

A few symbols will clarify these interrelations. N and L are the short-term interest rates in New York and London, both expressed as decimals and on a per-quarter rather than per-year basis. S and F are the spot and three-months forward exchange rates in dollars per pound sterling. The premium (or, if negative, the discount) on the forward pound is $p = (F - S)/S$. Arbitrageurs have no incentive to expand or shrink their commitments when one dollar plus New York interest for three months just equals one dollar's worth of spot sterling plus London interest for three months reconverted into dollars at the forward rate. In symbols, then,

$$1 + N = \frac{1}{S}(1 + L)F$$

Noting from the definition of p that $F/S = 1 + p$ and rearranging, we obtain $p = (N - L)/(1 + L)$, or $p = N - L - pL$. Since p and L are ordinarily both small decimals, their product, pL, is negligibly small. To a close approximation, then, the interest-parity condition becomes

$$p = N - L$$

We obtain the same result if we consider arbitrageurs who begin and end in sterling rather than dollars. The formula corresponds to the usual verbal statement of the interest-parity condition, already illustrated in our examples: the rate of forward premium or discount on the pound approximately equals the positive or negative excess of New York over London interest rates. More generally, one country's currency stands at a forward premium or discount against another currency according to how much lower or higher interest rates are in the first country than in the second.

The simplification of dropping pL from the formula is only a minor reason why the equilibrium condition does not hold precisely true in reality. A more important reason is vagueness about *which* short-term interest rates to compare between countries; so many different rates prevail on different kinds of deposits, loans, and money-market paper. The rise of the Eurodollar or Eurocurrency market in the 1960s (see the appendix to Chapter 7) further complicates matters: interest rates in the United States and the United Kingdom are no longer the only ones relevant to dollar-sterling exchange rates, since many European banks will now accept interest-bearing deposits and grant loans in dollars and sterling as well as in their home currencies. The relevant borrowing and lending rates may be slightly different for different arbitrageurs. An arbitrageur may not be able to borrow as much as he might want at a given rate of interest: as he tries to borrow more, lenders may ask a higher rate. Bank credit rationing may pose vague limits to the promptly available supplies of arbitrage funds. Actual or feared restrictions on capital movements, as well as "moral dissuasion" by the authorities, may also let forward premiums and discounts deviate from their calculated interest parities. In deciding whether or on how large a scale to operate, arbitrageurs must also consider the expenses and opportunity costs of their operations. Still another complication is that assets and debts denominated in various currencies may give their holders various intangible advantages and disadvantages besides explicit interest.

In reality, under free-market conditions, these complications only slightly blur but do not upset the main implication of the interest-parity theory: discrepancies between forward and spot exchange rates are normally about as small as the interest-rate differentials between countries. Whatever the specific interest rates compared, these differentials are ordinarily no larger than a very few percentage points a year (and one fourth that much per quarter). The cost of forward-exchange protection against exchange risk is correspondingly small; and that cost may just as well be negative as positive, since the forward rate may deviate in either direction from the spot exchange rate at which the risk-avoider would have had to deal otherwise.

DEPARTURES FROM INTEREST PARITY

Under certain conditions, the discrepancy between forward and spot rates can unmistakably be either smaller or larger than interest parity would indicate. Narrow limits to the permitted range of spot fluctuation, if completely trusted, will constrain forward premiums or discounts. If people are sure that the dollar spot rate on sterling will not be allowed to rise above $2.42 or fall below $2.38, no one will contract to buy forward sterling for more than $2.42 or sell it for less than $2.38, regardless of how big the interest differential between New York and London might be. A forward rate outside the spot limits would prove that people did *not* completely trust their being maintained.

Extreme and one-sided distrust in maintenance of pegged spot rates could make forward premiums or discounts exceed interest-rate differentials. In quiet times, many medium-sized and small firms neglect to cover all their future commitments in foreign currencies. But when suspicion develops that their own currency will be devalued, their banks will warn them to cover future payments in foreign currencies by forward purchases. Exporters earning foreign exchange will be more inclined than ever to neglect selling it forward, hoping to sell it for a higher spot price after devaluation of their own currency. Foreigners committed to future receipts or payments in the suspected weak currency will have special incentives to sell it forward or neglect buying it forward. Outright speculators, as well, would sell it forward. Supply and demand could match on the forward market only at a rate well below the still supported spot rate. A currency considered a candidate for upward revaluation, conversely, could stand at a large forward premium from its spot rate. At such times, limits to arbitrage funds promptly available, especially if coupled with obstacles or discouragements to their movement, would keep interest arbitrage from holding forward discounts or premiums in line with interest parities.

Things are different with a freely fluctuating spot rate. It cannot be as one-sidedly expected to rise or fall as can a precariously pegged rate. Furthermore, it can join in the mutual adjustment of all forward and spot rates and interest rates to the interest-parity relation. Speculation could conceivably dominate spot and forward rates alike; but even then, they would move together as described by the interest-parity theory.

In short, the interest-parity principle describes the close relation between forward and spot rates most accurately for freely fluctuating rates and least accurately for pegged spot rates that are either completely trusted or one-sidedly distrusted. History provides some striking examples of abnormally large forward discounts or premiums at times of heavy bearish or bullish speculation on pegged but distrusted spot rates. Episodes like these must underlie the common misconception that a *general* susceptibility to large discounts or premiums keeps forward-exchange contracts from being a cheap and dependable way to avoid exchange-rate risk. Ironically enough, as Professor Egon Sohmen has noted, the forward-spot discrepancies so characteristic of the present system of adjustably *pegged* spot rates are often cited as evidence of the costliness or impossibility of risk avoidance under *flexible* rates. With similar irony, arguments against flexible rates often stress the observed thinness of markets in long-term forward exchange, even though that thinness stems partly from actual or feared official restrictions on interest arbitrage amidst the balance-of-payments troubles so characteristic of the present system.

ARBITRAGE AND MARKET BREADTH

The existence of the forward-exchange market helps fill temporary, random imbalances between supply and demand of spot exchange that might otherwise perhaps cause sharp and functionless temporary wobbles in flexible exchange rates. For example, a depreciation of that sort in a currency's spot value would lead arbitrageurs to buy that currency spot while selling it forward, thus tending to sustain its spot value. This is not to say that forward-exchange transactions persistently resist all exchange-rate movements, regardless of how fundamental their nature. The point, rather, is that arbitrage links all spot and forward markets and money markets at home and abroad together, making each one less thin and the prices in it less sensitive to random shocks than we might infer from the volume of transactions in it alone. Arbitrage increases the actual or potential volume of transactions in each of the linked markets, making the market broader and more resilient than it would be in isolation. In this respect, the arbitrage linking spot, forward, and money markets resembles the international arbitrage in securities that was observed to have a stabilizing influence in foreign-exchange markets in the late nineteenth century. A sudden random depreciation of the Austrian gulden, for example, would make internationally traded securities quoted on the Vienna stock exchange appear cheap in comparison with the same securities quoted abroad. Arbitrageurs would leap at the chance to export securities at a profit, and their activity would tend to check the gulden's depreciation. Of course, these market-broadening effects of arbitrage presuppose essentially complete freedom for international capital movements of various types.

REFERENCES

1. LELAND B. YEAGER. "A Rehabilitation of Purchasing-Power Parity." *Journal of Political Economy,* LXVI, December 1958, pp. 516–530.

2. BELA BALASSA. "The Purchasing-Power Parity Doctrine: A Reappraisal." *Journal of Political Economy,* LXXII, December 1964, pp. 584–596.

3. PAUL EINZIG. *A Dynamic Theory of Forward Exchange.* London: Macmillan, 1961.

4. EGON SOHMEN. *The Theory of Forward Exchange.* International Finance Section, Princeton University, 1966.

INTERNATIONAL
SETTLEMENTS
AND LIQUIDITY

MONEY IN INTERNATIONAL USE

Since the late 1950s there has been much discussion of whether a shortage of "international liquidity" exists already or is likely to develop in the future and whether the present sources of international liquidity are satisfactory. Newspapers and magazines keep repeating the idea that as world income and world trade continue to grow, countries will need more and more international liquidity for financing trade and for making payments to each other.

Such language personifies "countries" in an unacceptable way unless the user makes it clear just what his metaphors really mean about the actions of individual persons, business firms, commercial and central banks, and other governmental and international institutions.

Actually, individual persons and business firms carry on international trade. They finance their operations through ordinary commercial banks. In the Western world it is the exception rather than the rule for governments to conduct trade. Exporters and importers quote and agree to prices and receive and make payments in ordinary national currencies. They use the currency of the exporting or importing country, or of some third country. Bank loans to finance imports and credits granted by exporters are likewise expressed in and repayable in national currencies. The moneys used in domestic and international transactions alike typically take the form of bank deposits. Some currencies, notably the dollar and the pound sterling, enjoy especially wide use in international transactions, but these so-called "vehicle currencies" nevertheless remain the ordinary money of particular countries. National currencies exchange for one another on the foreign-exchange market, and none of the ordinary private participants in the market deals in any distinctive kind of international liquidity.

Deficiency of a country's domestic money supply has a comparatively clear meaning: if severe, it would show itself in deflation of employment, production, and prices. At present, governments and central banks generally have the ability and the will to prevent any such deficiency. But what could a deficiency of international liquidity mean? Quite a few of the newspaper and magazine writers who blithely refer to the growing need for liquidity to match the growth of trade and settlements between countries are open to the suspicion of not really knowing what their metaphors mean. Some apparently do not realize that there is anything to be explained when they write of countries' trading with one another, of having to pay each other, and of sometimes running deficits and surpluses and having to make and receive settlements. Even academic economists, who presumably do understand their own shorthand language, all too often fail to tell their readers just what they mean when they write of "official settlements" between "countries," of "settling deficits" or "settling debts" that have arisen between "countries," and of various proposed rules about the use in these "settlements" of the new "international liquidity" to be created under certain plans for reform.

Actually, the supposed need for international liquidity to finance imbalances or make international settlements refers to the need that central banks or governments feel to hold reserves of gold and foreign currencies with which to intervene on the foreign-exchange markets to keep exchange rates fixed when the rates come under the pressure of imbalances in private transactions. "Official settlements," as the term is used in the contexts mentioned, are generally connected with official exchange-rate pegging.

GOLD

Under the traditional gold standard, governments and central banks refrained from regular intervention on the foreign-exchange markets. They usually stabilized exchange rates indirectly, instead, by maintaining two-way convertibility between their own currencies and gold. With the minor exception of some actual foreign-exchange operations since 1961, the United States still does maintain the exchange-rate stability of the dollar in this indirect way (though with the further exception of restricting convertibility into gold to dollars held by foreign and international monetary authorities). Most countries, however, maintain exchange stability by dealing directly on the foreign-exchange market in their own and foreign currencies. They do not intervene with gold itself because gold is not one of the items traded on the foreign-exchange market.

What, then, could the familiar statement mean (here quoted in the words of Miroslav Kriz) that "Gold remains the ultimate means of settling balances among the principal trading nations"? Under a regime of bilateral payments agreements such as prevailed widely in the early years after World War II, and even under the European Payments Union of 1950–1958, such statements could bear a fairly literal interpretation. Central banks routinely made short-run advances to each other to supply the currencies demanded on the market at fixed exchange rates. At the times of periodic settlements, central banks that had run up net debts to their partners would make full or partial settlement, as agreed, by transferring United States dollars or gold, either bilaterally or through the intermediary of the European Payments Union. But nowadays, central banks no longer routinely develop debts to and claims on each other for directly stabilizing the exchange rates between each two currencies, and the terminology of "official settlements" ordinarily no longer applies in the literal sense. Ordinarily, each country's authorities just keep its currency from appreciating or depreciating against the United States dollar (or, for some countries, the pound sterling). The stabilization of all other exchange rates is left to private arbitrage. A deficit country's central bank no longer typically makes payment to or obtains an advance from a surplus country's central bank; instead, the one simply runs down and the other builds up its own holdings of dollars. Each deals not with the other specifically but with the general run of transactors on the interbank foreign-exchange market.

Under these circumstances, loose references to the use of gold in international "settlements" must mean the sale of gold for the dollars a central bank needs to intervene with on the foreign-exchange market in support of its own currency. The central bank might sell the gold to the United States Treasury, to the International Monetary Fund, to some other central bank that happened to have a surplus of dollars for which it wanted gold, or to the general run of buyers on the London gold market.

> In times of emergency, of course, central banks may still lend to each other, especially by activating bilateral "swap" agreements of the kind mentioned on page 102 below. An inter-central-bank debt could also arise and be settled as in the following example: The Federal Reserve Bank of New York, acting as agent for the Bank of England, buys sterling with dollars to support it. The Bank of England later takes over the sterling bought for it, paying with gold. But these transactions amount to the same thing as if the Bank of England had first sold the gold for dollars and then itself used the dollars on the foreign-exchange market.

Because of its ready salability for the dollars they actually use in supporting their own currencies on the foreign-exchange market, central banks find gold an attractive asset in which to hold their external reserves, their "international liquidity." The central banks of the major West European countries, like the United States itself, do in fact hold the bulk of their reserves in gold. But none holds gold alone. They want some dollars as working balances for use in the very near future. Furthermore, they can invest their dollar reserves at short term and earn interest, while gold itself is sterile. Still another reason is that the United States exerts pressure on foreign authorities not to rock the boat of the international monetary system, as they supposedly would do if they converted too many of their dollars into gold.

Why don't central banks go to the other extreme and hold all or practically all of their external reserves in dollars (or sterling), especially since they could then earn interest? The old gold-standard tradition of holding actual gold is part of the answer. Furthermore, taking a loss on gold seems practically impossible, apart from storage costs and the loss of interest, while holding gold might conceivably bring a profit (or avoid a loss). Especially in view of American balance-of-payments deficits, no central banker worries that the dollar price of gold might be officially cut. Discontinuing the monetary use of gold and letting it find its free-market price as an ordinary commodity (perhaps below its present official price) also seems out of the question. There is no limit to how far the United States could go in keeping *up* the dollar price of gold; it could simply create dollars in any necessary amounts (a standard procedure) to buy all the gold offered to it at the present price. Central bankers likewise repudiate all thought of increasing the price of gold, although gold-mining interests do call for an increase. Some and perhaps most supporters of a return to a quasi-automatic gold standard also advocate a substantial increase; they realize that at the present price, gold stocks and annual gold production available for increases in official reserves would be too small for gold to perform the expanded monetary role that they would assign to it. There *is* an objective limit, furthermore, to how long the United States could persist in holding *down* the price of gold: if its stock were to run out completely, it could no longer continue selling gold to hold down its price.

The limited capacity of the United States to hold the price of gold down but its unlimited capacity to hold the price up, together with existing policies and attitudes, put gold in the position that a corporation's stock would have if it were guaranteed against going down in price but might possibly rise. For investors, that feature might well outweigh the disadvantage of the stock's not paying dividends.

FIRST- AND SECOND-CLASS
INTERNATIONAL MONEYS

This one-way-only adjustability of its price makes gold what J. M. Culbertson has called "first-class international money." It is the reserve medium that central bankers prefer, the substance for which they regard reserves of dollars or sterling as mere "second-class" substitutes. When the gold value of a reserve currency comes under serious suspicion, central bankers are inclined to dump that substitute and scramble for the safety of gold itself (except as they restrain each other by agreements and arm-twisting). Private hoarders behave similarly. In 1966 and 1967, for example, gold production made no net addition to the reserves of monetary authorities; instead, slightly more gold than was produced went into industrial uses and private hoards.

Paradoxically, almost everybody discusses whether or not "the dollar is as good as gold"; few people even think to ask whether gold is as good as the dollar. Yet the dollar, not gold, is the chief "vehicle currency" used in private trade and financial transactions and in official exchange-market intervention. The dollar is the home currency of the world's chief banking center and capital market, New York. Even borrowers outside the United States now float bond issues denominated in dollars for sale to other non-Americans. Besides this European market in dollar bonds, the Eurodollar market (described in the appendix to this chapter) illustrates the dominance of the dollar in international finance. Although the United States has by no means fully succeeded in preventing price-level inflation, the dollar has retained more of its purchasing power in the past ten or twenty years than almost any other currency. Gold fares no better in purchasing power as long as it remains tied to the dollar at a fixed price, and gold-holders receive no interest as an offset to any loss. The dollar's good—relatively good—record seems likely to continue. One element of strength, perhaps minor, is that the United States is less exposed than most countries to imported inflation and the inflationary bias of existing international monetary arrangements (see pages 66–67, 116–120 and 139–140), since the foreign-trade sector of the American economy is so small in relation to the whole.

The dollar's second-class status is not only paradoxical but also artificial. The asymmetry of expectations about the dollar price of gold results from United States gold policy. It contributes to the United States balance-of-payments deficit that has bred uneasiness about the adequacy of the country's gold reserves. A vicious circle is operating: the weakness of the dollar, artificial and policy-induced though it is, contributes to the deficit, while the deficit contributes to the weakness. Since about 1960, outflows of capital have been a major element in the United States deficit and have provoked the controls mentioned in Chapter 4. Short-term capital has flowed out heavily at times, notably in the fall of 1960 (dramatized by the great spurt in the price of gold on the London market that October), in the last quarter of 1964 (shortly before and apparently in anticipation of the imposition of "voluntary restraint"), and apparently after the British devaluation of 1967. Quasi-speculative considerations may have influenced even the outflow of long-term investment capital: the possibility of dollar devaluation or tighter controls gives potential American investors in foreign securities or business properties an extra reason for not procrastinating. At least, that is how Professors Triffin and Machlup have persuasively interpreted recent experience. If they are right, the capital outflows that have figured so heavily in the United States deficit have been spurred by an element of one-way-option speculation against the dollar, stemming in turn from the one-way movability of the price of gold.

The dollar would shed its paradoxical, artificial, policy-induced second-class status and its true strength would come to the fore if the United States made it quite clear that it no longer promised to buy unlimited amounts of gold at the existing floor price—if, for example, it warned that once its gold stock ran out, it would not only cease selling gold but would also cease standing ready to buy it. Such a declaration would fit into only one or two rather unpopular schemes that have been proposed for the reform of the international monetary system. Before describing those proposals and their more popular rivals, we should further examine the existing system.

MORE ABOUT GOLD

To summarize: Gold enjoys its preferred status as a reserve medium because it can readily be sold for the dollars actually used in official market interventions and because prevalent policies and beliefs make a fall in its price even more unlikely than a rise. Members of the International Monetary Fund (described later in this chapter) are required to pay part of their subscriptions to the Fund in gold and to declare par values of their own currencies in terms either of gold itself or of the dollar as its gold "content" was defined in 1944 (and still is defined); this amounts to the same thing in practice as declaring parities in terms of the dollar. Gold's role as "a common denominator of currencies" is an incidental aspect of exchange-rate pegging.

In only a few countries, notably the United States, did the law still require gold as domestic monetary reserves. In March 1965 the requirement for a 25 percent gold reserve was repealed for the deposit liabilities of the Federal Reserve Banks and left in effect only for Federal Reserve notes. The required percentage had already been reduced in 1945. Eroded as it had become, the domestic reserve requirement remained little more than a symbolic link with the time of an actual gold standard. Not since early 1933 has United States money been domestically redeemable in gold. Although the spontaneous tendency of purchases and sales of gold by the United States Treasury is to expand and contract the supply of "high-powered" domestic bank reserves, the Federal Reserve ordinarily does not allow these spontaneous tendencies to prevail. It offsets them by open-market operations, managing bank reserves by criteria other than the country's gold stock. (In this respect the Federal Reserve is in a better position than the central banks of small countries whose foreign trade, balances and imbalances of payments, and losses and gains of gold or foreign-exchange reserves do bulk large among the factors affecting domestic high-powered money.) It is true that at times since around 1960, United States monetary policy has been tighter than it would have been if there had been no balance-of-payments problem, but it has not been as tight as it would have been if the gold losses had been allowed to have their full contractionary effect. Offset as they have been, the gold losses have merely caused the Federal Reserve at times to keep the growth of the country's domestic bank reserves and money supply slower than otherwise. Furthermore, the precedents of 1945 and 1965 suggested that whenever the gold reserve requirement became domestically cramping, it would be further relaxed or would be removed. In fact, it was removed in March 1968. Gold no longer has any real domestic monetary significance.

Yet gold is often called the ultimate form of liquidity. Unlike paper claims, it has physical substance and direct usefulness and desirability of its own; it is no one's debt. It meets the traditional specifications of an ideal money material—durability, identifiability and standardizability, divisibility, portability (smallness of bulk in relation to value), and the others. It is relatively immune to inflation. (Inflation can occur under the gold standard. Between 1896 and 1910, United States wholesale prices rose 50 percent. But governments cannot simply print gold as they can print paper money in vast amounts.) Throughout the ages, gold has commanded confidence. It serves as a universally desired, readily exchangeable form of wealth, one easier to protect than bank accounts, securities, and conspicuous tangible assets from confiscation by a tyrannical government. Refugees from tyranny can take gold along with them relatively easily. With some such ideas in mind, presumably, no less modern an economist than Sir Roy Harrod [*Reforming the World's Money,* pp. 80, 172] has called gold "a sheet anchor of liberty," "a bulwark of human freedom." Partly because of these properties, gold seems to be the moniest money, the real thing for which paper money and bank deposits are mere supplements and substitutes.

Ironically enough, it is precisely the attempt to preserve a key role for gold in modern monetary systems, or the pretense of doing so, that has deprived gold of most of whatever serviceability of the kinds just mentioned it ever did have. One of the traditional arguments for the gold standard was that it fostered a state of affairs in which an economy had to adjust itself to an objectively given quantity of money, largely immune to the machinations of politicians and special economic interests. Yet in fact, governments have sought to loosen the link between the quantities of gold and money. They have devised or tolerated methods of "economizing" on gold. Money has increasingly been pyramided onto a relatively narrow gold base by such measures as the withdrawal of gold coins from circulation in favor of a gold bullion standard, by the spread during the 1920s of the practice of basing domestic money on a fractional reserve of foreign money, in turn only fractionally based on gold, by neutralizing the impacts of gold inflows and outflows on domestic money supplies, and by prohibiting private gold ownership since the 1930s. Inconsistently, nations have tried both to preserve and to escape the linkage of money to gold. They have tried to preserve an appearance while destroying the substance. So doing, they have destroyed, among other things, the role of gold as "a bulwark of human freedom." At present, possession of gold not only fails to enhance a person's freedom but makes him liable to criminal prosecution.

THE PRESENT GOLD-EXCHANGE STANDARD

The existing international monetary system certainly is not a gold standard. Instead of directly maintaining two-way convertibility between their own currencies and gold, most countries simply peg their exchange rates with one of the "key" or "reserve" currencies, dollars or sterling, and hold part of their official reserves in that currency. Monetary authorities outside the United States enjoy the privilege of two-way convertibility between dollars and gold at the United States Treasury. For this and other reasons, the system is often called a "gold-exchange standard."

Although gold still constitutes the bulk of official reserves, the foreign-exchange component has been gaining ground. Between the ends of 1948 and 1966, 57 percent of the *increase* in total gold and foreign-exchange reserves held by noncommunist countries (not counting drawing rights at the International Monetary Fund) has consisted of foreign exchange. For noncommunist countries other than the United States, 72 percent of the increase in their reserves over the same period has either consisted of foreign exchange or corresponded to United States gold losses. New gold production in noncommunist countries, together with Russian gold sales in the West, has accounted for only a small fraction of the growth in reserves. New gold supplies are inadequate by themselves—especially with so much of the new gold going into private hoards—to satisfy the reserve demands of monetary authorities. To satisfy them under the existing system, therefore, the supplies of key currencies available to monetary authorities must grow, which implies that the key-currency countries, notably the United States, continue to run deficits.

THE INTERNATIONAL MONETARY FUND

No description of present arrangements for international liquidity should overlook the International Monetary Fund. The IMF is an important focus of the international cooperation necessary for a workable system of adjustably pegged exchange rates. It was negotiated at the Bretton Woods Conference of 1944 and was ready for business in 1947. Each member of the Fund is obliged, with some exceptions, to avoid controls over the use of its currency in current international transactions, to convert balances of its currency held by the monetary authority of another member into either the currency of the member making the request or into gold, to declare a par value of its currency in gold or in dollars worth $\frac{1}{35}$ of an ounce of gold, and to peg the exchange rate of its currency within 1 percent of parity. (A member that stands ready to buy gold from and sell gold to foreign monetary authorities at appropriate fixed prices, as the United States does, is deemed to be satisfying this last requirement.) Exchange-rate adjustments are authorized only to remedy "fundamental disequilibrium" in the country's balance of payments.

When running a deficit not "fundamental" enough to require an exchange-rate adjustment, a member country should continue supporting its currency on the market by drawing on its reserves. To supplement skimpy reserves or to convince speculators on a devaluation that they cannot win, the member may seek assistance from the IMF. The assistance comes in the form of the currencies of other members, which the deficit country can use like its own reserves.

The amounts of assistance available, as well as voting power in the Fund, are defined in relation to each member's *quota*. Its quota is determined according to such factors as trade, national income, and international payments. Normally, a member has contributed 25 percent of its quota in gold and 75 percent in its own currency. When it draws from the Fund, it buys other countries' currencies and pays additional amounts of its own into the Fund. Up to the equivalent of the 25 percent of its quota paid in gold (its "gold tranche") a member may buy other currencies virtually at will. If drawings by other members have reduced the amount of one member's currency held in the Fund to less than the original 75 percent of its quota, its virtually automatic drawing right is enlarged by the difference in question. Beyond this so-called "super gold tranche" (if any) and its "gold tranche," a member has further drawing rights, known as "credit tranches," whose total amount equals its quota. Since a member draws foreign currencies by buying them with its own, its maximum total drawing rights are conveniently described by saying that the Fund should not hold the member's currency in an amount greater than 200 percent of its quota. (At that limit, the Fund would be holding the member's currency in amounts corresponding to the 75 percent of its quota originally subscribed in that form plus the 25 percent gold tranche and the 100 percent of credit tranches.) The Fund may waive this limit to drawings, however, and sometimes has. Especially liberal drawing privileges have also been introduced in favor of primary-producing countries troubled by temporary shortfalls in their export earnings. As the Fund's practice has evolved, a member enjoys the "overwhelming benefit of any doubt" in being allowed to draw on its gold tranche. This is one reason why the Fund encourages its members to regard their unused gold tranches as part of their international liquidity, along with gold and foreign-exchange reserves. A member can further count on very sympathetic consideration of an application to draw on the first of its four equal-sized credit tranches. Drawings on the remaining credit tranches are subject to increasingly close scrutiny of the member's efforts to solve its payments problems but are likely to be permitted when they would, as the Fund says, "support a sound program aimed at establishing or maintaining the enduring stability of the member's currency at a realistic rate of exchange." By attaching strings to its aid, the Fund may exert leverage on behalf of anti-inflationary financial policies within member countries.

Sometimes a mere "standby agreement" is aid enough: the Fund promises the member to supply it with foreign currency if necessary during the life of the agreement. The agreement makes the member feel freer to support its currency with its own reserves and helps discourage bearish speculation.

The rules of the IMF and the availability of its aid are supposed to promote freedom from exchange controls, convertibility of currencies (in the modern sense described on page 15), and multilateral rather than bilateral balancing of trade. Under these conditions, an applicant for aid has no special desire to draw the specific currencies of the countries with which it happens to be running bilateral deficits. It is concerned with its overall payments position and with shoring up the general foreign-exchange value of its currency; what it wants from the Fund is foreign exchange in general in the form of the currency it routinely uses in intervening on the market. For most countries, this means dollars. The Fund holds the currencies of all its members, however, and not only dollars. At present, therefore, the Fund usually supplies aid in a package of several currencies. The ones included are the currencies of countries whose strong payments positions or ample dollar reserves of their own enable them conveniently to supply dollars in exchange for their own currencies that the aid-receiving country has just drawn from the Fund.

A member that has drawn on the Fund is expected to repay its drawing as soon as convenient, and in any case within three to five years. Technically, the member "repurchases" its own currency, with which it had initially "purchased" foreign currency. Often, however, a member is said to "borrow" foreign currency in the first place and to "repay" this "loan" later. This informal language comes naturally, for the Fund's operations do resemble lending to distressed members. A member's repurchase obligation is reduced, however, to the extent that other members purchase its currency from the Fund.

The foreign currency with which a debtor repurchases its own is not necessarily the one drawn in the first place. Drawings must be repaid in gold or in currencies acceptable to the Fund, and a currency will not be acceptable if the Fund already holds it in excess of 75 percent of the quota of the currency's home country. In 1964, when this restriction barred repayments in dollars, the United States made its own first drawing on the Fund. It drew foreign currencies that were acceptable in repayments and sold them for dollars to countries which would otherwise have redeemed their dollars at the United States Treasury for gold with which to repay the Fund. By drawing on the Fund (and paying the required service charges), the United States escaped the drain on its gold stock that would have resulted because of the technicality just mentioned.

The Fund gained resources with which to aid its members by general increases in quotas and subscriptions in 1959 and 1966, by special further quota increases for many countries, and by the General Arrangements to Borrow, ratified in 1962. Under the General Arrangements, the "Group of Ten" (the Netherlands, Belgium, Germany, France, Italy, the United Kingdom, Sweden, the United States, Japan, and Canada), together with Switzerland (not a member of the Fund), agreed to lend up to a total of $6 billion of their own currencies to the Fund when needed for relending to fellow participants. (Not all of the $6 billion would be available at once, of course, since a country would not both borrow and lend under the General Arrangements at the same time.) Such a scheme is no substitute for curing a "fundamental" balance-of-payments disequilibrium, but it could help foil a bear raid on a major currency by convincing speculators that huge defensive resources were available.

OTHER SOURCES OF INTERNATIONAL LIQUIDITY

The International Monetary Fund is not the only source of finance for temporary imbalances. The European Fund is an organ of the European Monetary Agreement, which succeeded the European Payments Union at the end of 1958; on a smaller scale it grants its members short-term currency-stabilization loans much as the IMF does. Since 1962 the central banks of the major industrial countries have developed a network of bilateral "swap" agreements whereby each partner stands ready to supply its own currency temporarily to the other when needed to defend one of their currencies on the market. The Bank for International Settlements in Basel, Switzerland, provides a certain amount of coordination. The BIS had already helped work out the so-called Basel Agreements whereby central banks cooperated to cope with the speculative capital movements that followed the German and Dutch revaluations of March 1961. The BIS had been established in 1929 to administer a program of handling World War I German reparations. During the 1950s it operated the European Payments Union, and since 1958 it has played a similar role in the European Monetary Agreement. It also accepts gold on deposit from European central banks and governments and trades in gold, spot and forward, on the London gold market. It continues to serve as fiscal agent of various international government loans and plays host at regular meetings of central bankers.

Owned reserves and formal or informal drawing rights are not the only kinds of international liquidity that countries may have available for supporting their currencies. Forward-rate policy may provide a supplement or partial substitute. If a currency is important enough to be actively traded on the forward-exchange market, the authorities of its home country may sometimes usefully intervene on that market. By making contracts on a large scale to buy their own currency (sell foreign exchange) forward, the authorities can keep speculative pressure from pushing the currency's forward quotation to a sizable discount. Vigorous enough forward intervention can make outward covered interest arbitrage (see pages 83–85) unprofitable and can induce bearish speculators to sell the currency at its supported forward rate rather than sell it spot. The forward intervention thus takes pressure off the spot rate and lessens the reserve losses necessary to defend it. Since the forward intervention consists merely of making contracts for future transactions, it currently entails no drain on reserves; and if the policy is still succeeding by the time the contracts come due, the authorities' deliveries of foreign exchange under their contracts are more or less matched by their receipts of it as operators who must deliver the home currency under their maturing contracts obtain it by selling foreign exchange on the spot market. By its very nature, forward intervention of this sort is useful only for defense against a speculative attack that is quite unrelated to any fundamental disequilibrium and that is fated to reverse itself. The policy simply helps keep an otherwise appropriate and tenable exchange rate from collapsing merely because the reserves are small in relation to the volume of speculation. The advantages and dangers of such a policy are the topic of academic writings too numerous to summarize here.

Drawings on the International Monetary Fund, like similar expedients, are to be used for supporting currencies in the face of balance-of-payments deficits, not for financing development projects. (Indirectly, though, the IMF may aid economic development by providing expert financial advice.) Granting long-term development loans is the main job of the Fund's sister institution, the International Bank for Reconstruction and Development ("World Bank"), also chartered at the Bretton Woods Conference of 1944. The World Bank grants loans only to agencies of its member governments or to private borrowers backed by government guarantees. Its affiliate, the International Finance Corporation, makes nonguaranteed loans to medium- and small-sized private enterprises. Another affiliate, the International Development Association, makes "soft" loans for projects that could not meet the rather banker-like criteria for loans from the World Bank itself. Other international development-financing agencies include the Special United Nations Fund for Economic Development, the Inter-American Development Bank, the Asian Development Bank, the African Development Bank, and the European Investment Bank (an agency of the Common Market). The Export-Import Bank of Washington, the Agency for International Development, and other United States government agencies also play a role in financing development in backward countries.

THE SPIRIT OF THE EXISTING SYSTEM

Let us survey some of the broad ideas underlying the IMF or Bretton Woods system as a whole. The first—based on a debatable interpretation of experience in the 1930s—is horror of fluctuating exchange rates and competitive exchange depreciation and faith in fixed exchange rates bolstered by deliberate international cooperation. A second is the supposed distinction between temporary balance-of-payments disequilibriums, stemming from accidental or random disturbances and requiring no drastic corrective action, and infrequent "fundamental" disequilibriums, presumably reflecting deep-seated and persistent maladjustments that warrant exchange-rate adjustments. How to make that distinction currently, without hindsight, has never been clearly explained. A third idea, that of deciding on exchange-rate adjustments only after thorough international consultation and expert appraisal, proved unrealistic because of massive one-way-option speculation while adjustments were actually or even only supposedly under consideration. A fourth key idea, also now discredited, was the hope that governments could control disruptive capital movements effectively while leaving normal current-account transactions free. Fifth was the hope that convertibility of currencies at fixed exchange rates (convertibility for nonresidents, at least) could be rapidly achieved, making a centralized clearing machinery, as well as exchange controls on current account, unnecessary.

The International Monetary Fund shares the job of trying to relax trade and payments restrictions with the General Agreement on Tariffs and Trade, a curious hybrid of multilateral treaty and international organization. Besides coordinating negotiations for tariff cuts, the GATT embodies a set of rules (riddled, however, with exceptions) against discriminatory trade policies, quantitative trade restrictions, export subsidies, and undue customs complexities. The IMF campaigns against currency and payments restrictions. The division of responsibility between GATT and IMF is rather artificial, due largely to historical circumstances at the times they were negotiated, since import barriers and exchange controls often serve the same purposes and differ only in administrative details.

In the actual course of events, most IMF members clung to the Fund's postwar-transition-period excuse for retaining exchange controls for many years beyond the time the controls were originally expected to lapse. The European Payments Union, established in 1950 to cope with some of the deficiencies of the early IMF system (and succeeded by the European Monetary Agreement at the end of 1958) deserves much of the credit for finally weaning its members away from drastic trade and exchange controls. The decontrol trend of the 1950s, following the widespread currency devaluations of 1949, came at a time when European countries were generally running balance-of-payments surpluses and were willing to add more worth of dollars than of gold to their reserves, while the United States was willing to run deficits because its gold reserves were still so large. Although, as Walter Salant has said, "the system seemed to do well in making the major currencies increasingly acceptable when controls were in operation, it became less adequate as soon as they were removed. The removal of controls and other factors, such as the growth of trade, have increased imbalances." In the 1960s, significantly enough, even such major countries as Great Britain and the United States backslid into controls to cope with balance-of-payments troubles.

After near-inactivity during its first decade, the International Monetary Fund staged a spectacular rescue of sterling at the time of the Suez crisis in 1956. Since then its bold, large-scale activity has achieved several further rescues of currencies. Those episodes hardly prove the success of the IMF system, however, if the system itself tends to breed opportunities to display such heroism.

The management and staff of the IMF deserve praise for their competence and for the advice and moral support on behalf of domestic financial prudence that they give to officials of less advanced member countries. The Fund conducts scholarly research and issues publications of high quality and great usefulness. A broader appraisal, however, must tie in with an appraisal of the whole system of international liquidity and adjustably pegged exchange rates that the Fund defends and symbolizes. An assessment of its future development must tie in with proposals and prospects for international monetary reform.

REFERENCES

1. FRITZ MACHLUP. *International Payments, Debts, and Gold.* New York: Charles Scribner's Sons, 1964. Essays X through XIII.

2. MIROSLAV A. KRIZ. "Gold in World Monetary Affairs Today." Reprinted from *Political Science Quarterly,* December 1960, as pages 84–99 in Finn B. Jensen and Ingo Walter, editors, *Readings in International Economic Relations*; New York: The Ronald Press Company, 1966.

3. J. M. CULBERTSON. "U. S. Policy and the International Financial System." Pages 329–378 in *Recent Changes in Monetary Policy and Balance-of-Payments Problems,* Hearings before the Committee on Banking and Currency, House of Representatives, U. S. Congress, July 1963.

4. ROBERT Z. ALIBER. *The Future of the Dollar as an International Currency.* New York: Frederick A. Praeger, 1966.

5. ROBERT TRIFFIN. *The Balance of Payments and the Foreign Investment Position of the United States.* Essay No. 55; International Finance Section, Princeton University, 1966.

6. FRITZ MACHLUP. "World Monetary Debate—Bases for Agreement." Reprinted from *The Banker,* September 1966, by International Finance Section, Princeton University, 1966.

7. GUNTHER RUFF. *A Dollar-Reserve System as a Transitional Solution.* Essay No. 57; International Finance Section, Princeton University, 1967.

8. SIDNEY E. ROLFE, with the assistance of Robert G. Hawkins. *Gold and World Power.* New York: Harper & Row, 1966.

9. IAN SHANNON. *International Liquidity, A Study in the Economic Functions of Gold.* Chicago: Henry Regnery Company, 1966.

10. FRANCIS CASSEL. *Gold or Credit?* New York: Frederick A. Praeger, 1965.

11. ROY HARROD. *Reforming the World's Money.* New York: St. Martin's Press, 1965.

12. *International Financial Statistics.* Published monthly by the International Monetary Fund; contains statistics on gold and foreign-exchange reserves, among others.

13. FRANK A. SOUTHARD, JR. "International Monetary Arrangements." In J. Carter Murphy, ed., *Money in the International Order*; Dallas: Southern Methodist University Press, 1964, pp. 34–50.

14. FINN B. JENSEN and INGO WALTER, eds. *Readings in International Economic Relations.* New York: The Ronald Press Company, 1966. Selections 17 and 18 (on the International Monetary Fund).

15. SHIGEO HORIE. *The International Monetary Fund.* New York: St. Martin's Press, 1964.

16. INTERNATIONAL MONETARY FUND. *Annual Reports.*

17. BANK FOR INTERNATIONAL SETTLEMENTS. *Annual Reports.*

18. WALTER S. SALANT. "Does the International Monetary System Need Reform?" In J. Carter Murphy, ed., *Money in the International Order*; Dallas: Southern Methodist University Press, 1964, pp. 3–33.

APPENDIX: THE EURODOLLAR MARKET

An active market in foreign-currency deposits arose in London in the late 1950s and expanded in the 1960s. This development illustrates at least two things: the dominance of the dollar in international finance and the rapid adaptability of financial institutions on the international scene as well as within countries.

The term "Eurodollar" is hard to define because it so often serves as a loose label for a range of operations rather than the name of a specific thing. If forced to give a narrow definition, we might say that Eurodollars are deposits held with British or Continental banks but expressed in dollars instead of the local currency. Actually, banks in Canada, Japan, and other countries have also been accepting deposits denominated in United States dollars; and deposits in sterling and a few other European currencies are accepted by some banks outside the home country of each of these currencies. Still, "Eurodollar" (or "Eurocurrency") remains the usual label for operations of this sort. Even the term "deposits" may be slightly misleading, since banks with foreign-currency liabilities, far from having just passively accepted deposits, have actively borrowed in this form to obtain funds for relending.

A simplified example will help explain the system. A European has acquired a dollar deposit in a New York bank or has received a dollar check. He wants to continue holding dollars for a while, neither spending them nor converting them into his home currency. Instead of having to hold the dollars on deposit in New York, he can hold them in the form of a dollar deposit claim on his European bank, to which he transfers ownership of the deposit in New York. The European bank can in turn transfer this deposit to someone who wishes to borrow immediately spendable dollars. The European bank will hold such positions with many customers at the same time, owing dollars to many depositors and holding dollar claims on many borrowers. The bank will not lend away the full amount of United States bank balances transferred to it. It will keep a fraction of them in reserve to pay off depositors who may wish to cash their demand deposits or (more typically) their maturing time deposits into dollars actually spendable in the United States. Except for the fractional reserve held against its dollar deposit liabilities, the Eurobank has intermediated transfers of the dollar balances in the United States from its depositors to borrowers, while leaving its depositors still holding claims they regard as dollars. In a sense, the Eurobank has taken part in *creating* dollars. When we consider Eurobanks in the aggregate or as a system, we realize that their multiple creation of Eurodollars on the basis of additional reserves of United States dollars must be much more narrowly limited than the multiple creation of demand deposits on the basis of additional domestic reserves by the American banking system. Since Eurodollars do not circulate as an actual medium of exchange, the drainage of United States dollars out of the possession of the European banking system is relatively much larger than the analogous drainage of reserves out of the American banking system. In this respect, the operations of Eurobanks in creating Eurodollars and serving as intermediaries in loans of United States dollars resemble the operations of nonbank financial intermediaries in the United States, which create liquid (but also noncirculating) claims against themselves and serve as intermediaries in loans.

What motivates this system? Why should anyone care to hold Eurodollars? The chief reason seems to be that a depositor can earn a competitive interest rate on his Eurodollar deposit, whereas in the United States the Federal Reserve forbids interest on demand deposits and limits interest on time deposits. The Eurobank's motive is that it can relend the dollars at a higher rate of interest than it pays. The source of the interest-rate advantage shared between the Eurobank and its borrowing customer is the opportunity to borrow dollars relatively cheaply from a depositor whose alternative would have been to hold his demand or time deposit at no interest or low interest in the United States. Similar reasons partly explain transactions in Eurosterling and in deposits of Continental currencies outside their home countries: they help banks get around cartel agreements and other formal and informal domestic restrictions on interest rates. The more competitive international money market also provides scope for letting interest rates in large wholesale transactions reflect economies of scale. Furthermore, the familiar advantages of financial intermediation enter into the explanation. A European without regular American banking contacts can borrow dollars from his bank at home. Lenders of dollars—and these have often been American banks—can let better-placed European banks bear the trouble and risk of lending to ultimate European borrowers. The advantages of intermediation also help explain why several banks may stand in a long chain between the ultimate lender and the ultimate borrower, the banks inside the chain accepting dollar deposits from some banks and placing dollar deposits with others. Intermediation also provides opportunities to share or reallocate risks and tailor loans to the requirements of borrowers and tailor deposits to the requirements of depositors. Because of the law of large numbers, for example, dollars received on short-term deposit may be relent at longer term.

West European businesses and banks are by no means the only participants in the Eurodollar market. From about 1963 until the Johnson Administration imposed "voluntary restraint" in 1965, much of the Eurodollar supply consisted of funds lent by corporations in the United States. In the early stages of the market's development, especially, banks of communist countries acted on their supposition that dollars were safer from legal attachment or restriction when on deposit in a European than in an American bank. The central banks of many countries are also thought to have fed the Eurodollar market at times by holding parts of their external reserves in that form.

How is this new development to be appraised? The Eurodollar market "plays an important and constructive role in providing additional means for arbitrage," according to Paul Einzig, the leading authority on the subject; it "has greatly contributed towards increasing and redistributing the world's international liquid resources." It has helped meet the growing demand for credit to finance international transactions. For good or ill, it is a long step toward a keenly competitive and unified international money market. It has impaired the effectiveness of official restraints on interest-motivated international flows of short-term money. Business firms and banks have become more able than before to weaken or circumvent a domestic anti-inflationary tight-money policy by borrowing abroad and forcing their country's central bank to create additional "high-powered" domestic bank reserves as it buys up the borrowed foreign money to keep the exchange rate pegged. With this in mind, some observers have called the system "an international Federal funds market." Some say it blurs the definiteness of the size of a country's national money supply. At least, it does complicate the task of monetary management under fixed exchange rates. Some governments, including the American, have responded by tightening controls over international capital movements.

Critics of the gold-exchange standard may view Eurodollars as a new basis for their fears. They form a new layer in the inverted pyramid of various kinds of money and near-money onto a narrow ultimate gold base. Should confidence in fixed exchange rates and the fixed price of gold ever weaken, the scope for a destructive chain reaction would be greater than before the development of Eurodollars. As the Eurodollar market continues changing rapidly in its details, observers continue finding much material both for satisfaction and for alarm.

REFERENCES

1. FEDERAL RESERVE BANK OF RICHMOND. "The Euro-Dollar Market," *Monthly Review,* April 1967, pp. 8–10.

2. PAUL EINZIG. *The Euro-Dollar System.* 2d Ed.; New York: St. Martin's Press, 1965.

3. PAUL EINZIG. *A Textbook on Foreign Exchange.* New York: St. Martin's Press, 1966. Chapter 14.

4. ERNEST BLOCH. *Eurodollars: An Emerging International Money Market.* The Bulletin of the C. J. Devine Institute of Finance, New York University, No. 39, April 1966.

8

INTERNATIONAL MONETARY PROBLEMS AND PROPOSALS

ADJUSTMENT AND CONFIDENCE

The last chapter broached some features of the existing system that have engendered proposals for reform. Three problems have come to the fore. The first concerns *adjustment*. No automatic mechanism of international payments adjustment—neither the gold-standard mechanism nor the exchange-rate mechanism —is allowed to work continuously. Governments wait and hope that disequilibriums will either go away of their own accord or, given enough time, will ultimately yield to mild influences on wage-and-price trends. Occasionally, when prodded into action by crisis, governments will adopt *ad hoc* measures affecting trade and capital movements and may even modify domestic monetary and fiscal policy.

The lack of an adjustment mechanism contributes to a second problem: shaky *confidence* in the exchange rates at which currencies are pegged. When a country's balance-of-payments deficit persists, capital movements through one-way-option speculation are likely to aggravate the deficit.

LIQUIDITY

The vulnerability of currencies to losses of confidence contributes to a third problem, that of international *liquidity*. The great attention given this problem has diverted attention from the really crucial problem of adjustment. An adequate adjustment mechanism would largely avoid the problems of confidence and liquidity. International liquidity is the external reserves and drawing rights that governments and central banks hold for supporting their currencies on the foreign-exchange market. As world production and trade grow over the long run, and all the more so as prices continue in an inflationary trend, the absolute sizes of supposedly temporary deficits to be financed by drawings on liquid reserves will increase also. There are even some reasons (not necessarily conclusive ones) for expecting imbalances to increase more than in proportion to the total money value of trade. Technology and productivity are advancing and demands are shifting; yet the necessary adaptations within both deficit and surplus countries often must be slow because they require transferring capital and labor among industries. As trade becomes freer, if it does, and as the industrial countries draw closer together in technology, productivity, per capita incomes, and consumer tastes, changes in relative costs are likely to exert their influence over a broadened range of actual and potential trade. Trade balances are likely to become more sensitive to international price differences. Walter Salant further argues that as wealth increases, as liquid balances held privately for trade and other purposes grow, and as financial markets become more closely linked, capital movements may well magnify the volatility of overall balances of payments.

No definite relation exists between objective magnitudes such as volume of trade or deficits experienced in the past and a "needed" volume of reserves. A country's reserves must be either large enough or growing fast enough to forestall anxiety over them; otherwise, its government may slide into controlling trade and capital movements. The anxieties of government officials and central bankers are perhaps not quite as foolish as they appear in Fritz Machlup's amusing comparison of their attitudes with Mrs. Machlup's passion for a huge or rapidly growing wardrobe. Reserves do have to be comfortably larger than any nonspeculative drain on them is likely to be if confidence is to endure, for losses of confidence and of reserves reinforce each other. Even otherwise huge reserves could prove inadequate to defend a currency in the face of fundamental disequilibrium interacting with loss of confidence. But if the exchange value of a currency is approximately correct, huge reserves discourage the speculative capital outflows that might otherwise draw them down and so make themselves look all the more huge in relation to actual drawings on them. Either skimpiness or hugeness tends to exaggerate itself through the behavior of speculators, which is one more reason why there can be no simple and dependable relation between the size and the adequacy of a country's reserves. This vagueness about how much international liquidity is "enough" for a single country is just one reason for doubting that the present international monetary system provides a world total that is right in any definite sense.

TRIFFIN'S DIAGNOSIS AND PLAN

Professor Robert Triffin has vigorously criticized existing liquidity arrangements. Despite the impressions created by some of his early writings on the topic, his worry is not that the world already faces a shortage of international liquidity. Mainly he worries about how haphazardly its growth is determined and about the "absurd" (as he says) nature of the sources of that growth. Existing sources of reserve growth are undependable and plagued with contradictions. The fundamental absurdity is the use of national currencies as international reserves. The bulk of the postwar reserve growth of countries outside the United States has consisted of gold lost by the United States and the buildup of American liabilities to foreigners. While the continuing United States deficits are necessary to provide this growth in the international liquidity of other countries, they are also alarming. The United States gold reserve shrinks not merely as a percentage of the growing foreign liquid claims pyramided against it but even in absolute amount as foreign authorities convert into gold some of the dollars they acquire in pegging exchange rates. Curing the United States deficit would improve shaky confidence in what has been the chief element of growth in international liquidity, foreign-held dollars, but would restrict their supply.

Triffin proposed a way out of this dilemma: a new international money would be created, perhaps in the form of deposits with a reformed International Monetary Fund, for use among central banks. As time went on, countries would hold more and more of their international liquidity in this new form, displacing dollars and sterling. A central bank needing another country's currency for exchange-rate stabilization could buy it with the new IMF money from the other country's central bank. The IMF could create its new money by lending to members with balance-of-payments deficits, by buying national securities or the bonds of international development banks, or by giving it to member countries outright according to some formula. The total supply of this "paper gold" supposedly could be regulated to grow at some appropriate moderate pace. No longer would international liquidity grow erratically according to the vagaries of gold production, industrial gold consumption, private gold hoarding, gold sales by the Soviet Union, the balance-of-payments positions of the key-currency countries, and the willingness of central banks to hold key currencies rather than redeem them in gold.

Unfortunately, not even a powerful international agency would find it easy to keep the supply of liquidity just right. The main difficulties would come in trying to manage it on the national and international levels both. Liquidity created to remedy a supposed international shortage might well not be needed to remedy any domestic deflations. However, the opposite conflict is unlikely—too much liquidity to lubricate international trade at pegged exchange rates (whatever an excess for that purpose might mean) but not enough to prevent deflation within countries. Domestic policy can avoid domestic deflation. The conflict is asymmetrical: a shortage of international liquidity does not significantly restrict domestic money supplies, yet creating more of it may well expand them inappropriately. In line with its very purpose, additional liquidity allows deficit countries to run larger and longer-lasting deficits than they otherwise would, without correcting them by deflation, devaluation, or controls; and this puts inflationary pressure on the countries with the corresponding surpluses. To the extent that surplus countries succeeded in neutralizing imported inflation, they would further thwart balance-of-payments adjustment. If the international authority, reluctant to feed inflation, guided itself by money-supply requirements within countries, only coincidence would assure adequate reserves for exchange-rate pegging. Even on the national level, monetary requirements diverge among countries. An international authority could not ensure adequate but not excessive national money supplies, as well as adequate external reserves, all at the same time.

MODERATE SUBSTITUTES FOR THE TRIFFIN PLAN

This rather subtle point is not the reason why government officials and central bankers greeted the Triffin Plan with suspicion. It simply looked too radical. Various supposedly more acceptable substitutes were invented to remedy the absurdities Triffin had diagnosed in the key-currency-reserve system. One early counterproposal would have had the key-currency countries cure their balance-of-payments deficits, yet continue supplying their own currencies as international liquidity by buying foreign currencies to hold as part of their own external reserves, along with gold. The dollar, while still a reserve medium for foreign countries, would itself be backed partially by reserves of foreign currencies. *Business Week* once called that scheme "monetary incest." Another idea was to multiply the sources of liquidity growth by agreement for central banks to hold their reserves in *several* currencies in at least roughly specified proportions. This idea of a "composite reserve unit" could be formalized by having countries deposit their own currencies in an international pool, receiving in return international units matched in specified proportions by the currencies deposited. Alternatively or in addition, countries could multiply the sources of currencies available for exchange-market intervention in time of crisis by perfecting the patchwork system of bilateral and multilateral standby loan agreements that has in fact been extensively developed since 1961 and 1962. A further alternative or supplementary approach would be to increase members' quotas in the International Monetary Fund again, as they have been increased in the past. The Fund's statutes could be modified to make as much as desired of each country's borrowing rights—and not just the gold tranche—available without questions asked. Furthermore, these rights would no longer have to be regarded as borrowing rights: they could come to be regarded as deposits in the Fund that their holders would own outright and could draw down without obligation to reconstitute them. Additional amounts of such deposits could even be credited to the members' accounts periodically as the world's "need" for liquidity grew, and without any longer requiring the members to give the Fund supposedly equivalent amounts of their own currencies in exchange. The new IMF deposit money would not have to be redeemable in anything. It would simply circulate in a closed circuit among central banks; each would agree to accept it in payment for its own money supplied to fellow members wanting it for intervention on the foreign-exchange market (or for conversion into the dollars actually to be used in interventions). The new international money would play essentially the same role as gold nowadays.

One might object: Why oblige a surplus country to accept this money when it might already have more international liquidity than it wanted and might even be plagued with a problem of imported inflation? Theoretically, the only limit to the amount of "paper gold" that a member might find itself called upon to accept would be the total amount of it held by all the other members. (Of course, the chance of reaching that limit is infinitesimal.) But much the same is true under a full-fledged gold standard or even under today's gold-exchange standard: a country leaves itself open to receive, at the limit, all the gold held by other countries. The problem of a surplus country under a system providing enough international liquidity to make exchange-rate pegging feasible for most countries is essentially the same regardless of just what serves as the reserve medium.

PROSPECTS FOR REFORM

In reviewing alternative reform proposals, we have worked back to something resembling the Triffin Plan itself. Official discussions have drifted this way. At the International Monetary Fund meeting in Rio de Janeiro in September 1967, the delegates agreed on the essentials of a plan to be drafted as amendments to the Fund's charter and submitted to the member governments for ratification. Under the name of "special drawing rights," paper gold would be created from time to time and distributed to members in proportion to their IMF quotas. A deficit country could transfer some of this new asset to other countries to obtain their currencies or (more typically) dollars for sale on the foreign exchange market in support of its own currency. Which countries were called on to accept the special drawing rights in such transactions would be determined by rules akin to those now governing the choice of currencies to be drawn from the Fund in its present lending operations (see page 101). The new asset would carry a gold-value guarantee and earn a moderate rate of interest, and certain rules would also prod member countries to accept and hold it. Even after ratification by the IMF members, the plan could go into actual operation only with the approval of members holding at least 85 percent of the voting power. Like the Triffin Plan, the new system would face the question of the proper amount of international liquidity to be created. What amount could be enough by some criteria without being too much by others? Does the concept of an optimum amount of international liquidity even have any meaning?

In the new system that Professor Triffin had already said he expected to evolve eventually, sterling and dollars would continue to be held as working balances for private trade and investment and for routine central-bank interventions in the foreign-exchange market. But central banks would increasingly convert foreign exchange acquired in excess of actual working balances into claims on an international institution such as the IMF. (To keep desires for actual gold reserves from destroying the system, gold holdings would have to be held down voluntarily or by agreement.) The international institution would in turn convert the sterling and dollars it acquired into medium- or long-term claims on the United Kingdom and the United States. Those claims would not be cashed disruptively for speculative reasons.

We should remember, though, that the Triffin Plan and similar reforms all would deal mainly with the liquidity problem and to some extent with the confidence problem but hardly at all with the adjustment problem. Providing more ample resources for pegging exchange rates is hardly a method of correcting balance-of-payments disequilibriums. Admittedly, more adequate finance for larger and longer-lasting deficits would impose stronger pressures of imported inflation on countries with the corresponding surpluses; and if the result were a still more definitely inflationary bias in the world economy than already prevails, countries with deficits would have a better chance to cure them merely by lagging behind for a while in the worldwide inflationary procession. This rather unappealing solution directs our attention to a wider range of alternative types of international monetary system.

REFERENCES

1. FRITZ MACHLUP. "World Monetary Debate—Bases for Agreement." Reprinted from *The Banker,* September 1966, by International Finance Section, Princeton University, 1966.

2. WALTER S. SALANT. "Does the International Monetary System Need Reform?" In J. Carter Murphy, ed., *Money in the International Order;* Dallas: Southern Methodist University Press, 1964, pp. 3–33.

3. FRITZ MACHLUP. "The Need for Monetary Reserves." Reprinted from *Banca Nazionale del Lavoro Quarterly Review,* September 1966, by International Finance Section, Princeton University, October 1966.

4. HERBERT G. GRUBEL, ed. *World Monetary Reform.* Stanford, Calif.: Stanford University Press, 1963.

5. ROBERT G. HAWKINS, ed. *Compendium of Plans for International Monetary Reform.* The Bulletin of the C. J. Devine Institute of Finance, New York University, No. 37–38, December 1965.

6. ROY HARROD. *Reforming the World's Money.* New York: St. Martin's Press, 1965.

7. ROBERT TRIFFIN. *The Balance of Payments and the Foreign Investment Position of the United States.* Essay No. 55; International Finance Section, Princeton University, 1966.

A BROADER RANGE

OF ALTERNATIVES

ALTERNATIVE EXCHANGE-RATE SYSTEMS

The reform proposals reviewed so far aim at shoring up the present system of pegged exchange rates by contriving a sounder basis and a less haphazard growth of international liquidity. This chapter and the next consider the present system as just one among a broader range of alternatives. In describing the actual and supposed advantages and disadvantages of each, the chapters will refer to some earlier analysis, particularly of balance-of-payments adjustment; but they amount to more than a review.

None of the alternative systems is to be rejected merely because it has disadvantages. They all do; none is perfect. A sensible choice among them cannot be made by comparing the lengths of lists of arguments pro and con; some supposed advantages and disadvantages are spurious and some are unimportant, and any debater can increase or decrease the number of arguments by dividing or consolidating. A sensible choice requires trying to understand how the whole economic system would work under each of the exchange-rate alternatives and comparing the desirabilities of these "big pictures."

The following survey tries to give a fair account of the major points made by economists of different persuasions. Unavoidably, though, it is written by an author who has reached a judgment of his own—one subject to revision, but rather definite at the time of writing. The reader will soon see what this judgment is (if he does not know already); and, for the sake of balance, he should pay particular attention to contrary views, not only as summarized here but especially as presented by economists who hold them. A reader seriously interested in the controversy will find a good start in the items numbered 2, 3, 10, 11, 12, and 13 in the references at the end of this chapter.

Either a return to a genuine international gold standard or adoption of freely fluctuating exchange rates would provide a really radical reform. In some respects these two systems stand at opposite poles, but in one respect they stand together: both would allow market forces to equilibrate balances of payments in relatively automatic ways. Both stand opposed to efforts to escape adjustment or to making adjustment depend on *ad hoc* governmental decisions or direct controls.

THE GOLD STANDARD

A genuine gold standard would tie national currencies together by having each redeemable in and obtainable for gold at a fixed and supposedly permanent price. Gold ownership and gold shipments would be unrestricted. Maintaining the fixed relation to gold would necessarily become the overriding aim of each country's monetary and fiscal policy; national money supplies and price and income levels would have to conform to the requirements of balance-of-payments equilibrium at fixed exchange rates.

A genuine gold standard would put an end to the present awkward hybrid character of international liquidity. Countries would hold their reserves entirely in gold and no longer in key foreign currencies. The price of gold in terms of all currencies would almost certainly have to be raised at the time of return to a gold standard, supposedly for that one last time. Otherwise, the money values of gold stocks and current gold production would be inadequate for the expanded role of gold. Thereafter, however, a gradual and continuing process could theoretically sidestep the problem of the adequacy of liquidity. Adjustments in price levels would keep real (purchasing-power) quantities of gold and gold-based national currencies adequate to meet demands for international liquidity and for domestic cash balances. Under the historical gold standard, as Sir Roy Harrod benevolently described it, "The linkage of gold to the domestic circulation . . . meant that, if the increase in gold stocks was not keeping pace with the growth of world production and trade, the domestic circulations would not keep pace either, and there was a tendency for prices to fall." If the number of ounces of gold held by central banks "did not keep pace with the growth of world trade, the value of world reserves might none the less keep pace, because the value of each ounce tended to rise." The firm link and substantial overlap between national and international moneys and the quasi-automatic adjustment of balances of payments would resolve any inconsistency between the amounts of money needed within countries and internationally.

The more fully currencies coincided with gold alone instead of being based on merely fractional reserves of gold, the more nearly would the quantity of money be determined by objective conditions and be immune from the influences of politics and of self-seeking economic interests. Money supplies and, as a result, business conditions would be more stable than they have been under nongold currencies as typically managed in actual experience.

This argument blends with an argument about the anti-inflationary discipline of the gold standard. Lax inflationary policies would promote imports, hamper exports, threaten exhaustion of the gold reserves, and so force the monetary authorities to mend their ways. Domestic redeemability of all money in gold coin would contribute to the discipline by reminding the authorities that any policies likely to weaken confidence in the currency might well touch off a run from the currency into gold. That very danger would even check inflationary policies in the first place.

Exchange-rate stability under the gold standard favors international trade and investment. Short-term capital movements reinforce this stability, since speculators know that exchange rates will not move appreciably outside the gold points. The gold standard, coupled with its supposed corollaries of free trade in goods and services and freedom of movement of capital and persons, promotes world economic integration. Anyway, these are the arguments.

On the other hand, the gold standard faces one tremendous obstacle. The smooth operation of its balance-of-payments mechanism and the smooth adjustment of each country's real money supply to the requirements of a growing economy presuppose an unrealistic degree of price and wage flexibility. When deflation becomes necessary to remedy or prevent a balance-of-payments deficit or to compensate for an otherwise inadequate growth of gold supplies, prices and wages will not absorb the entire impact; and until prices and wages do eventually adjust downward, employment, production, and real incomes must suffer. A money supply linked tightly to the gold stock cannot adapt itself in any simple way to a country's long-run growth of population, productivity, and total productive capacity. If the gold stock does not grow in step, the need for downward adjustments in sticky prices and wages will hamper realization of the economy's growth potentialities. This is the likelier long-run tendency, although new sources and refining methods could conceivably produce the opposite difficulty of inflation.

OTHER FIXED-RATE SYSTEMS

The accidental determination of money supplies could conceivably be avoided by tying national currencies to reserves of a "paper gold" such as mentioned in Chapter 8. Alternatively, one particular national currency might even serve as the basis of the system, a possibility already hinted at earlier.

Thorough international financial integration would be conceivable under a fixed-rate system either with or without a gold basis. Professor James Ingram has recommended such integration. Trade in securities and other financial claims and transfers of capital and interest and dividends would be freed of all legal restrictions. Local and foreign securities would become thoroughly intermingled in the portfolio of the typical financial institution. A sizable part of the entire stock of financial claims held by a country's residents could potentially enter into international payments adjustment, and the adequacy of a country's external reserves in the strict sense would no longer be a serious problem. Exchange rates would require little central-bank support. As the customers of commercial banks in a deficit country drew down their deposits to make net payments abroad, individual banks would replenish their dwindling reserves by selling securities from their portfolios. Those sales would raise interest yields marginally in the deficit country, attracting foreign funds. Capital movements could become extremely sensitive to interest-rate differentials if exchange rates were completely and permanently rigid. Speculative foreign-exchange crises could not occur in the absence of fundamental disequilibrium. Avoiding disequilibrium would require close coordination among financial policies; no country could pursue a separate national monetary policy.

Except for the deliberate regulation of the size of its reserve base, a nongold system of permanent exchange rates could have all the essential properties, advantages, and disadvantages of a genuine gold standard. Only the position of the reserve-currency country, if a national currency rather than an international paper gold were the basis of the system, would have to be exceptional. Admittedly, the national or international managers of the reserve medium might depart from prudence, and governments might eventually loosen the ties of their own currencies to the reserve medium, but much the same is true of the gold standard itself: no monetary system can have foolproof and perpetual built-in guarantees against violation of its rules.

INTERNAL AND EXTERNAL BALANCE

Under fixed exchange rates, the discipline of the balance of payments will sometimes, by coincidence, be healthy. In a country suffering both a payments deficit and domestic inflation, considerations of both external and internal balance call for monetary-fiscal restraint or contraction. ("External balance" means balance-of-payments equilibrium; "internal balance" means "full employment without inflation," or, if that double goal is too ambitious, it means the compromise that is best on domestic grounds between full employment and price-level stability.) For a country with a payments surplus and a depression, the goals of external and internal balance would both recommend monetary-fiscal expansion. It is just as possible, though, for internal and external considerations to pull in opposite directions and for balance-of-payments discipline to be perverse. A country with depression and a payments deficit needs an expansionary policy for the first trouble but a contractionary policy for the second. A country initially enjoying both kinds of balance might be thrown into this dilemma by the contagion of a depression originating abroad. The opposite clash of policy requirements would plague a country with inflation and a balance-of-payments surplus. Inflation originating abroad might be the source of its trouble: theory and historical experience amply testify that inflation can be "imported" through a balance-of-payments surplus. The logic of the external adjustment mechanism under fixed exchange rates requires inflation, in fact, as a key element in correcting a surplus.

When a disturbance to internal and external balance originates at home, the financial policies required for internal and external balance coincide. When a disturbance originates abroad or in the foreign-trade sector of an economy, the internal and external requirements clash. In general, when a deflationary or inflationary disturbance originates within one country, the ideal financial policy, from home and foreign viewpoints alike, is correction at the source.

Even when a country's internal and external policy requirements coincide in *direction,* they may clash in *degree.* More precisely, they may begin to clash even in direction after policy has pursued both requirements to a certain extent. For a country sharing a world depression while running an export surplus, both internal and external goals call for an expansionary policy. But it would be extreme coincidence if the same degree of expansion were needed for both. On the one hand, a relatively slight export surplus might vanish while depression still lingered at home. Further treatment of the depression would throw the balance of payments into deficit. On the other hand, a relatively slight depression might be cured while an export surplus persisted. Further expansion to cure this surplus would spell domestic inflation.

Conflicts of direction and degree can arise when only one policy weapon, financial policy (policy designed to affect the total flow of expenditure on goods and services), is used for pursuing two goals. The problem is to hit two targets with a single shot. The feat is hardly possible unless the two targets happen to be perfectly in line with each other. That is conceivable. For example, expansionary financial policy might remedy a depression and improve the profitability of business so much that outflows of investment capital gave way to inflows, remedying a previous overall payments deficit even despite an income-induced rise in imports. But such fortunate coincidences cannot be counted on and would hardly persist anyway.

One conceivable solution to the two-targets problem is to split financial policy into the two separate weapons of monetary policy (interpreted as interest-rate policy) and fiscal (budgetary) policy. Both interest-rate manipulations and the government budget affect total spending and economic activity and thereby affect imports and exports also. Interest rates have an additional effect on international capital movements. Interest-rate policy thus has a comparative advantage, so to speak, in controlling the overall balance of payments, while fiscal policy has a comparative advantage in controlling domestic business conditions. A country with depression at home and a balance-of-payments deficit could conceivably solve its problem by adopting an expansionary fiscal policy combined with a tight monetary policy, while a country with the two opposite imbalances would adopt the two opposite policies. Except perhaps for mild and temporary clashes between internal and external requirements, though, this idea of splitting expenditure policy counts more as a piece of academic ingenuity than as serious policy advice. For one thing, the idea assumes away concern about the make-up of the balance of payments and tacitly regards a current-account deficit matched by an artificially stimulated capital inflow as just as satisfactory as a closer approach to balance in the two external accounts separately. Maintenance of capital inflow could become increasingly difficult as a larger and larger fraction of the total stock of internationally mobile funds had *already* moved. Payment of interest on a growing debt to foreigners could eventually become an important balance-of-payments debit item in its own right. This burden would be particularly regrettable if capital had been artificially lured in the first place from countries where its marginal productivity was relatively high to a country where its marginal productivity was relatively low. Furthermore, the government budget, the government debt, the money supply, interest rates, and rates of capital formation and economic growth are all interrelated. How strongly a budget deficit spurs total demand, for example, surely depends on how it is financed, which also affects interest rates. The performance of the home economy could suffer unless something distinct from monetary-fiscal policy helped serve external balance.

CAPITAL MOVEMENTS UNDER DIVERGENT PRICE TRENDS

Interest-sensitive capital movements and divergence of financial policies among countries pose a further possible difficulty under fixed exchange rates. Consider a country whose policies permit continuing price-level inflation while other countries maintain price stability. Expectations of continued inflation tend to show up in a so-called price premium by which the actual rate of interest exceeds the "real" rate. Then, although the real rate of interest and the real marginal productivity of investment were the same in the inflationary country as elsewhere (or even somewhat lower), that country could have a higher actual rate of interest and so attract funds from abroad. That flow of capital in response to a distorted interest-rate differential would presumably represent an international misallocation of resources. But would the flow actually occur? Wouldn't a sustained exchange depreciation of the inflationary currency discourage the flow fully as much as the interest-rate differential encouraged it? No; such an offset would tend to occur under free exchange rates but not under fixed rates that still commanded confidence. Exchange-rate pegging can keep a currency's internal and external values on rather different courses for some time. The very inflow of capital in question (not to mention controls and various *ad hoc* measures) could help sustain the pegged exchange value of the inflationary currency. In short, fixed exchange rates can promote counterproductive capital movements in at least one way (apart from speculation) not also characteristic of a free-rate system.

FREELY FLUCTUATING EXCHANGE RATES

But this is a minor argument. There is essentially only one main argument for free exchange rates, just as there is only one main argument—efficiency—for free trade. The exchange rate is the simplest balance-of-payments equilibrator, while alternative mechanisms require unpleasant changes in price levels or employment or breed restrictions on trade and capital movements. To work smoothly, the exchange-rate mechanism requires much less flexibility of local-currency prices and wage rates than does the price-and-income mechanism of fixed exchange rates. The necessary changes occur largely through translation of prices and wages from one currency into another at exchange rates that are inherently flexible (but not necessarily unstable) because they are determined continuously by supply and demand in a highly competitive market. The changes occur mainly where they are most relevant to external balance—in the prices of internationally traded goods. As explained in Chapter 5, free rates both facilitate necessary adjustments and avoid unnecessary ones.

Exchange-rate freedom permits aiming domestic policy squarely at internal balance, and with good prospects of success even in the face of depression or inflation in less well managed foreign economies. A few economists have even argued that free exchange rates would not merely relieve monetary policy of balance-of-payments complications but would actually make it more effective. Expanding the money supply and reducing interest rates to fight a recession, or even just letting interest rates fall spontaneously, as they typically do in a recession, tends to cause capital outflow. The balance of payments would move into deficit—except that the home currency depreciates on the exchanges enough to cause an export surplus of goods and services matching the capital outflow. This export surplus makes a timely addition to the total demand for domestic output and domestic labor and other factors of production. An anti-inflationary monetary policy, conversely, influences capital movements so as to make the home currency appreciate, bringing a net inflow of goods and services into the country and restraining any uptrend in domestic prices.

Free exchange rates do not, of course, *guarantee* sensible and mutually consistent policies affecting domestic aggregate demand and international trade and capital movements. Nothing can. But by banishing balance-of-payments complications, free rates at least permit such policies. That is the system's one great advantage.

The arguments against it are innumerable. Probably the leading one insists that the risk of loss from exchange-rate fluctuations discourages international trade and investment. This point ranks high on the list of arguments for the gold standard (yet price and employment fluctuations under the gold standard create business risks of their own). Trade and investment would flourish most of all under a system that kept exchange rates dependably fixed while preserving all the advantages of free rates. That statement is empty, though, for there is no such system. Actually, considerations of promoting trade and investment do not all run against the free-rate system. It makes tariffs and controls unnecessary for balance-of-payments purposes. Unless distorted by speculation—a worry considered shortly—free rates always tend toward equilibrium levels at which quantities of currencies supplied and demanded are equal on the foreign-exchange market and international transactions balance. As on any competitive market, the volume of transactions tends to be larger at equilibrium prices than at prices pegged too high or too low.

Forward-exchange facilities, furthermore, can provide protection against most of the exchange risk in international trade. The worry about the cost of this protection is largely mistaken. As Chapter 6 explained, forward-exchange contracts, instead of merely insuring against exchange risk at the price of an insurance premium, actually eliminate the risk by canceling opposite risks against each other. In fact, forward premiums and discounts are more likely to remain small, in line with interest parities, under free exchange rates than under alternative systems: interest arbitrage can be allowed freer scope, and the forward market can escape the one-sided speculative pressures that develop when pegged spot exchange rates come under strong suspicion. For long-term international loans and other commitments, admittedly, forward-exchange protection is not very practical; but this difficulty is hardly peculiar to free exchange rates. Over the long run, even pegged rates are subject to change; and price-level changes would pose analogous difficulties for long-term international—and domestic—commitments if otherwise sound domestic financial policies were subordinated to trying to keep exchange rates permanently fixed.

The familiar worry about disruptive speculation under free exchange rates is usually a priori and seldom goes beyond mere assertion. The historical evidence typically cited either concerns episodes of extreme inflation in which fixed rates had broken down or involves confusion between truly free exchange rates and the compromise systems considered in the next chapter. Flexibility expected to be only temporary also differs from a system of truly free rates. In the early and middle 1920s, for example, several depreciated European currencies were plagued by fluctuating beliefs about how imminent their intended return to prewar parity was. These beliefs responded to, as well as influenced, exchange rates. A currency's rise or fall on the market tended to strengthen or weaken hopes of its early repegging onto gold, which in turn reinforced the rise or fall. In the years around 1890, similarly, changing rumors about the adoption of the gold standard in Austria-Hungary and Russia occasionally contributed to speculative fluctuations of the paper gulden and ruble. An avowed policy of permanently free rates would avoid such influences.

The further argument that functionless exchange-rate movements shift labor and other resources wastefully back and forth between domestic-goods and international-trade-goods industries is really part of the speculation argument and not a distinct argument in its own right, for it could hardly be anything other than speculation that could make exchange rates move functionlessly, out of contact with changes in economic fundamentals. In one respect the free-rate system scores a point over compromise systems: it does not incite destabilizing speculation by presenting speculators with a one-way option.

EXPOSURE TO INFLATION

The monetary independence that free rates afford is an advantage from one point of view but a disadvantage from another. Independence means escape from the discipline of balance-of-payments crises that, under fixed exchange rates, would punish and perhaps even forestall inflationary laxness in domestic policy. Under fixed rates but not under free rates, a government can cite the danger of a balance-of-payments crisis when calling on labor-union leaders and businessmen patriotically to fight inflation. A free exchange rate provides no rallying point, as a fixed rate might, in support of guidelines and moral suasion designed to restrain excessively greedy wage demands and pricing policies and so shrink the wage-push element in inflation and improve the trade-off between unemployment and inflation.

Professor Robert Triffin has stressed a related advantage that the free-rate system lacks. Suppose that a previously stable country commits an inflationary mistake in domestic policy. Under fixed exchange rates, its inflationary impulses would spill out into spending on additional imports, whose availability and price competition would restrain price increases at home. The local price and cost structure would have suffered only minor damage by the time that losses of external reserves had forced the country's authorities to correct their inflationary mistakes. A free-rate system, on the other hand, would bottle up inflationary pressures within the country and allow them to raise the local-currency prices of foreign exchange, of imports, and of goods and factors of production in general. By the time inflationary mistakes had been corrected, it would be too late to prevent or reverse the damage; prices, and especially wages, would exhibit their characteristic downward inflexibility. In short, free exchange rates would give inflationary mishaps or mistakes full scope to push costs and prices irreversibly upward. The reactions of foreign-exchange speculators to the expectations generated by inflationary accidents would hasten the country's slide along the one-way road to currency depreciation.

Exchange-rate pegging, in contrast, permits the country to enjoy the anti-inflationary assistance of a balance of payments deficit: the real goods and services in effect borrowed from abroad help hold down prices, while the sale of foreign exchange drawn from official reserves or borrowed abroad may absorb money at home. The gearing of the home economy into a not-yet-inflated world environment provides time to correct inflationary impulses before they become irreversibly consolidated into wages and prices.

Although this happy result is conceivable, it is not clearly more typical than certain pro-inflationary tendencies (still to be described) that also sometimes operate under pegged exchange rates. And anyway, the desirable process now in question does not actually prevent all inflation. Rather, it makes inflation of local origin inconspicuous by diluting it onto the outside world. The inflating country shoves its problem onto other countries in small inconspicuous bits. It may use this opportunity to gain time while correcting its mistake—or it may not. For a while it may even reconcile the inflationary attempts of different economic groups to divide more than the total national output among themselves by meeting these excessive claims from external reserves already held or newly borrowed abroad. Each country is less immediately and fully exposed to the wanted or unwanted consequences of its own policies than it would be under the monetary insulation offered by fluctuating exchange rates. Such insulation would admittedly be a disadvantage for the less prudent countries but an advantage for the more prudent ones. Monetary independence under free exchange rates means freedom for prudence and recklessness alike.

For relatively prudent countries, the free-rate system may well have some anti-inflationary advantages of its own. For one thing, an incipient exchange depreciation of the home currency might warn effectively against any inflationary lapse responsible for it. Such a warning would be more conspicuous than reserve losses under fixed rates. More important, perhaps, the free-rate system lacks the long-run pro-inflation bias apparently characterizing the present adjustable-peg gold-exchange standard (described on pages 66–67, 140). Furthermore, the free-rate system makes controls unnecessary for balance-of-payments purposes. By thus permitting (though of course not guaranteeing) free trade and free international competition, the system would help maintain the discipline of competition over economic groups whose excessive wage and price demands might otherwise pose the familiar unemployment-or-inflation dilemma. Finally, freedom from balance-of-payments complications would facilitate (though again, would not guarantee) greater steadiness in domestic monetary-fiscal policies. There could be less of the zig-zagging between expansionary and contractionary policies that presumably contributes, in several ways, to a long-run inflationary bias.

Still, we must give the lack-of-discipline worry its due. Freedom from unhealthy external constraints also means freedom from healthy ones. If these constraints are *needed,* then, by assumption, so are fixed exchange rates. Free exchanges are no substitute for monetary discipline at home. In fact, the exchange-rate mechanism of payments adjustment would not work if the home money supply were out of control and rose in proportion to the price of foreign exchange whenever the home currency weakened on the foreign-exchange market. If a country cannot or will not maintain internal balance for itself and if it needs the anti-inflationary discipline of potential balance-of-payments crises at fixed exchange rates, then, by assumption, exchange-rate flexibility is inflationary in a permissive sense. Such a country might be well advised to try tying its own currency to some stable foreign currency.

The "discipline" argument for fixed exchange rates, and especially for the gold standard, appeals to people who mistrust their own governments. People who advocate free exchange rates despite the loss of external discipline do so partly because, as Professor Harry Johnson has suggested, they mistrust foreign governments even more than they mistrust their own; they fear monetary linkage with governments whose inflationary propensities may be even worse. The discipline argument seems most relevant for countries that have an intermediate propensity to inflate. The most inflationary governments are hardly restrained by fixed exchange rates; in fact, they cannot keep their rates fixed for long. Their currencies are pegged at disequilibrium rates most of the time: they are undervalued for a while after each devaluation but become increasingly overvalued again as inflation proceeds and makes another devaluation necessary. Wrongly pegged rates simply disrupt business without exerting effective discipline. At the other extreme stand the most prudent countries. Their resistance to inflation gains nothing from monetary linkage to foreigners. On the contrary, impulses of imported inflation may sometimes inconvenience them. In between stand the countries whose inflations are not fast enough to require frequent devaluations. Their pegged exchange rates do not become quickly and seriously wrong again after each (infrequent) adjustment. Yet they can benefit from external restraint on inflation. Applied to such countries only, the discipline argument is probably the strongest of the valid arguments for fixed and against free exchange rates.

THE TEMPTATION TO INTERVENE

One final argument against free exchange rates is that the system cannot endure. Sooner or later the authorities will feel the itch to "improve" on the operation of the free market, turning the system into one of manipulated flexibility or de facto adjustable pegging. History provides examples. But the difficulty is not inherent in the free-rate system as such: a policy of "hands off" the foreign-exchange market is perfectly clear and feasible if the authorities want to follow it. The considerations relevant to their decision is what a survey of the advantages and disadvantages of alternative systems is all about. If poor understanding were blocking a desirable policy, that fact would be no argument against trying to spread better understanding.

REFERENCES

1. International Study Group of 32 Economists, Fritz Machlup and Burton G. Malkiel, editors. *International Monetary Arrangements: The Problem of Choice.* International Finance Section, Princeton University, 1964.

2. ROY HARROD. *Reforming the World's Money.* New York: St. Martin's Press, 1965.

3. JAMES INGRAM. "A Proposal for Financial Integration in the Atlantic Community." Pages 177–207 in *Factors Affecting the United States Balance of Payments,* studies compiled for a subcommittee of the Joint Economic Committee, U. S. Congress, 1962.

4. J. E. MEADE. *The Balance of Payments.* London: Oxford University Press, 1951. Chapters VIII, IX, X.

5. ROBERT A. MUNDELL. "The Appropriate Use of Monetary and Fiscal Policy for Internal and External Stability." IMF *Staff Papers,* IX, March 1962, pp. 70–76.

6. RICHARD ABLIN. "Fiscal-Monetary Mix: A Haven for the Fixed Exchange Rate?" *National Banking Review,* IV, December 1966, pp. 199–204.

7. FRIEDRICH A. LUTZ. "Money Rates of Interest, Real Rates of Interest, and Capital Movements." In William Fellner and others, *Maintaining and Restoring Balance in International Payments*; Princeton University Press, 1966, pp. 161–166.

8. MILTON FRIEDMAN. Testimony favoring free exchange rates in *The*

United States Balance of Payments, Hearings before Joint Economic Committee, U. S. Congress, November 1963, pp. 451–459.

9. EGON SOHMEN. *Flexible Exchange Rates, Theory and Controversy.* University of Chicago Press, 1961.

10. [Ragnar Nurkse]. *International Currency Experience.* League of Nations, 1944.

11. Division of International Finance, Board of Governors of the Federal Reserve System. "A System of Fluctuating Exchange Rates: Pro and Con." Reprinted as pp. 57–70 in *Recent Changes in Monetary Policy and Balance-of-Payments Problems,* Hearings before the Banking and Currency Committee, House of Representatives, U. S. Congress, July 1963.

12. MILTON FRIEDMAN and ROBERT V. ROOSA. *The Balance of Payments: Free versus Fixed Exchange Rates.* Washington: American Enterprise Institute for Public Policy Research, 1967.

13. ROBERT TRIFFIN. Comments on pages 83 and 140 in National Industrial Conference Board Convocation (October 1965), *Gold and World Monetary Problems*; New York: Macmillan, 1966.

14. HARRY G. JOHNSON. *The World Economy at the Crossroads.* New York: Oxford University Press, 1965. (See page 28 for the observation cited.)

10

COMPROMISE SYSTEMS

CONTROLS

Several types of compromise between the two extremes of permanently fixed and completely free exchange rates have been adopted or proposed. In a way, resort to controls and other expedients at times of balance-of-payments trouble—special import-duty surcharges, "voluntary" restrictions on capital movements, and more forthright forms of trade and exchange control—represents an indecisive reluctance to choose between the adjustment mechanisms appropriate to fixed and to free exchanges. The main claim for controls is that they can deal with payments disequilibriums relatively quickly and surely, even when other methods of adjustment might be too slow and feeble.

On the other hand, controls are open to the same sorts of objections on efficiency grounds as are developed in the traditional analysis of protective tariffs versus free trade (and whatever qualifications apply to that analysis apply here also). We need not review all the arguments for and against controls, for their use does not represent a distinct system of international monetary relations. Instead, controls are expedients adopted to cope with deficiencies of some of the compromise monetary arrangements whose advantages and disadvantages we shall now survey.

THE CASE FOR THE ADJUSTABLE PEG

The best known compromise is the adjustable-peg or Bretton Woods system. It is the one now prevailing under the auspices of the International Monetary Fund (and already described in Chapter 7). It supposedly gives international trade and investment the benefits of exchange-rate stability except on the infrequent occasions of deliberate adjustments in rates. And on those occasions, the adjustment is quick and clean, instead of being stretched out into a long uptrend or downtrend. Adjustment of exchange rates to correct fundamental disequilibriums avoids the painful deflation of employment, production, and prices characteristic of correcting a deficit under the gold standard. Each country enjoys considerable freedom to aim its own monetary and fiscal policies at the best domestically achievable compromise between full employment and price-level stability. It need not sacrifice sound domestic policy to the balance of payments, since exchange-rate adjustment remains available to correct fundamental disequilibrium. Adjustments are expected to be rare, however. When external disequilibrium reflects a mere temporary disturbance and is fated to go away of its own accord, no disruptive change is necessary either in the exchange rate or in the home economy. Countries can simply "ride out" such disequilibriums, meanwhile building up or drawing down their external reserves and, if necessary, getting help from the International Monetary Fund.

DOUBTS ABOUT THE ADJUSTABLE PEG

This optimism presupposes that national monetary authorities have adequate reserves or borrowing rights. At this point the whole problem of the amounts and types of international liquidity, discussed in Chapter 8, comes to the fore. Perhaps an even more important damper on optimism is the question of how anyone can diagnose a disequilibrium as temporary or fundamental *until* either it actually has gone away of its own accord or else has persisted long enough to do damage. People understandably tend to wait and see, to hope that nothing much need be done until events have proved otherwise.

While exchange-rate stability as such promotes trade, stability *at disequilibrium levels* hampers it. The Bretton Woods system lets disequilibriums cumulate into occasional full-blown crises that finally provoke *ad hoc* policy responses, such as taxes and controls, interest-rate manipulations, and—infrequently—exchange-rate adjustments. One of the original purposes of the Bretton Woods system was to enlist international cooperation to avoid competitive exchange depreciation of the sort practiced during the depression-plagued 1930s, when countries tried to keep their currencies undervalued on the foreign-exchange market to promote exports and restrain imports and so stimulate employment at home, even at the expense of other countries. Postwar experience has turned out more nearly the reverse. Inflation has been much more usual than depression, and many countries have clung to pegs that overvalue their currencies. But since nobody knows how to calculate the correct new level when a peg is changed, countries tend to make their devaluations too large to be on the safe side. Actually, adjustment of pegs has fallen almost into desuetude nowadays. (Events *forced* the recent devaluation of sterling after long, costly struggles to avoid it had failed; Britain did not welcome that step.) The chief remaining corrective for payments disequilibrium is inflation in surplus countries and controls or other expedients in deficit countries.

Mention of this inflation bias is a partial (but not conclusive) answer to the claim that exchange-rate pegging exerts the anti-inflationary discipline also claimed for firmly fixed exchange rates.

Unfortunately, this discipline is even less likely to work surely and appropriately than under the gold standard. The Bretton Woods system seems to have an inflation bias because deficit countries, instead of deflating, can expect international assistance to help finance their deficits and can count on controls or devaluation as a last resort, while surplus countries tend passively to accept mild imported inflation. This is not to say that surplus countries are helpless against imported inflation or that the bias is a strong one, but such bias as does exist seems to run in the inflationary direction. Furthermore, balance-of-payments worries in the absence of a continuous adjustment mechanism complicate the pursuit of stability in domestic policy. The discipline of the balance of payments, especially as it works haphazardly and sometimes perversely under the adjustable-peg system, is a poor substitute for firm avoidance of inflation on properly understood domestic grounds.

Governments have become reluctant to adjust exchange rates for fear of undermining confidence and aggravating the problem of speculation. Even nowadays, with rate adjustment considered as practically a last resort, that problem is bad enough, since speculators realize that a country with a deficit may possibly be *forced* to devalue, however unwillingly. One-way-option speculation can occur not only in forthright ways but also through "leads and lags": importers in a deficit country who must make payments in foreign exchange and foreign exporters who have accepted payment in the deficit country's currency will hasten to complete their transactions before that currency drops in foreign-exchange value, while deficit-country exporters who have priced their goods in foreign currency will delay collecting or converting their foreign funds and foreign customers with debts in the deficit country's currency will stall off payment in hopes of devaluation. These shifts in timing amount to outward capital movements; they delay inflows into and hasten drains on the official external reserves of the deficit country. Shifts in timing may affect not only payments but also trade itself, hastening the deficit country's imports and delaying its exports. For a surplus country whose currency is considered a candidate for upward revaluation, such speculation runs in the opposite direction.

One-way-option speculation against wrongly pegged exchange rates sometimes disrupts the interest-parity relation between forward and spot rates (explained in Chapter 6). Further causes of abnormally large forward discounts or premiums at such times are one-sidedness in commercial covering against exchange-rate risks and interference with interest arbitrage by actual or threatened controls over capital movements. Since spot exchange rates are always subject to fluctuation within the support limits and may become subject to large adjustment at times of fundamental disequilibrium, cautious international traders cannot dispense with forward-exchange protection. To the extent that they make this protection less dependable or more costly, the sizable forward-spot discrepancies sometimes arising under the adjustable peg count rather seriously against that system. Forward-exchange facilities are less likely to have their good performance interrupted under free exchange rates.

Foreign monetary authorities as well as private holders may speculate against a currency by unloading it (perhaps for gold) when they fear its devaluation. Their restraint in doing so is, of course, one of the main types of international monetary cooperation at present. (Admiring emphasis on international cooperation under the adjustable-peg system amounts to backdoor recognition, incidentally, of the difficulties that require this cooperation.) *Guarantees* have been suggested as a way to reinforce cooperation. The United States, for example, would guarantee foreign official holders against loss in case it devalued the dollar; it would write up their dollar holdings to give the larger number of devalued dollars the same total value as before in gold or in the currencies of the holders. This idea does have considerable merit, and the objections that have been raised do not conclusively discredit it. One prominent objection is that it would be hard to confine the benefits of guarantees to foreign *official* holders. What, for example, would keep dollars from swarming into the guaranteed holdings of foreign authorities as private holders (even American holders) dumped them on the market and fled into other currencies? The prospect of large incalculable costs in their own currency would in some ways awkwardly tie the hands of the authorities giving a guarantee. Guarantees might make devaluations so costly that exchange rates would become frozen at their initial levels. Advocating guarantees may thus amount in practice to advocating permanently rigid exchange rates and abandonment of the adjustable peg.

MANAGED VERSUS FREE FLEXIBILITY

The world has also had some experience with a different compromise system. Managed flexibility means, ideally, allowing the exchange rate to keep a country's payments in equilibrium over the long run, but with an official exchange-stabilization fund (also called exchange-equalization account) in operation. The fund would trade routinely in the market to iron out fluctuations caused by any destabilizing speculation, random short-run mismatching of private supply and demand, and other temporary disturbances. Ideally, the system would reconcile domestic stabilization policy with exchange-rate stabilization, since the official operations would let the exchange rate maintain external balance, except in the very short run, by responding to the changing fundamentals of tastes, technology, weather, harvests, price levels, monetary and fiscal policies, and reasonable expectations about all of these. The fund would not resist fundamental rate trends. Its intervention would not mean any requisitioning and rationing of foreign exchange. The fund's open-market operations in foreign exchange would be as fully compatible with a free-market economy as a central bank's open-market operations in government securities.

This prospectus is attractive. But how are the fund's managers to distinguish promptly between fundamental rate movements and accidental or temporary oscillations around a relatively steady long-run average or trend? How can they know whether or not an observed movement is the start of a major shift in trend? Even speculation-induced rate movements may accord with the main trend, since speculators may be taking account of basic supply and demand conditions in international trade and of expected changes in them. Hindsight is not enough. If the fund's managers really were talented in diagnosing the present and foretelling the future, they could speculate profitably on their own private accounts and iron out temporary fluctuations without risking public money. But then, according to one argument, no official fund would be necessary. If the authorities possessed information not generally available to private speculators, they might best simply make this information public.

Even if the fund's managers could know (without waiting for

hindsight) that particular exchange-rate movements would prove purely temporary, it is far from clear that these movements would be functionless and should be blocked. Exchange-rate flexibility is a form of price flexibility, which has a role to play in continually adjusting production and consumption to changing circumstances. Keeping prices from fulfilling their rationing and production-motivating functions as conditions changed might prove more disruptive than the price fluctuations themselves. Even obviously temporary fluctuations, such as seasonal ones, can have a useful function. When nonstorable goods or the services of persons and property are involved and when a temporary slump in buying would let these go to waste, price stabilization could be particularly inappropriate. It would be a questionable idea to hold Florida hotel rates rigid all year long. The performance of a market is hardly to be judged by the degree of price stability it displays. If exchange-rate fluctuations would clearly be temporary or seasonal, private speculation would probably iron them out; but even if it did not, this failure would not necessarily be regrettable.

When official funds are at work in the market, exchange-rate determination becomes at least potentially a political matter. Governments may try to manipulate exchange rates toward disequilibrium levels for such purposes as improving terms of trade or stimulating employment (remember the "competitive exchange depreciation" of the 1930s). Different governments may operate at cross purposes from each other. Though exchange funds *may* serve as instruments of international cooperation, the very fact of official trading designed to influence rates gives scope for practices or at least accusations of nationalistic manipulation. An internationally owned and operated exchange stabilization fund, proposed by a few economists as a substitute for national funds, would presumably avoid these abuses; but even if the various diplomatic and administrative difficulties could be overcome, an international fund would still face most of the problems of national funds.

A policy supposedly confined to ironing out unwarranted fluctuations can drift into one of pegging rates at levels that ultimately prove wrong. This drift from smoothing into pegging was illustrated by several funds during the 1930s, including the British, and in several postwar Latin American experiences with supposedly fluctuating exchanges. If a fund holds a currency steady for months at a stretch, changing to a new level occasionally, speculators are likely to enjoy one-way options—and more often than under an avowed adjustable-peg system. Even if a fund manages to avoid actual pegging, it still may flag on the very speculation it is supposed to neutralize. To avoid giving speculators tips on a sure thing, it must keep at least some of its activities and intentions secret. But then speculators will guess. The idea of a "normal" exchange rate is less likely to prevail, with its stabilizing influence, when speculators must guess at the whims of an official agency not limited to profit-seeking than when they need consider only such fundamentals as price levels and interest rates and supplies and demands in international trade. In comparison with a free market, an officially dominated one involves more actual and suspected decisions and activities about which speculators' interpretations could suddenly change. Destabilizing speculation feeds on mysteries, gossip, and rumor. It is an open question whether a fund operating with enough self-restraint to avoid these dangers would really be missed if abolished.

In contrast with several historical examples of disruptively ambitious official intervention, there is one prominent example of a fund that seems to have neither engaged in pegging nor bred speculation about its own intentions. This is the Canadian Exchange Fund Account from October 1950 to about the end of 1960. At last, around the beginning of 1961 and most obviously in June, the Canadian authorities succumbed to the itch to manipulate the rate. From then until they fixed a par value for the Canadian dollar in May 1962, Canada illustrated the difficulties characteristic of a flexibly manipulated exchange rate. And *after* the repegging, a massive exchange crisis illustrated the speculative difficulties of the adjustable-peg system.

Ironically enough, many journalists and even some economists refer casually to the Canadian experience in 1961–1962 as illustrating the grave disadvantages of exchange-rate flexibility. In so doing, they ignore the fundamental distinction between a *free* exchange rate and a manipulated one. In important respects, a rate manipulated to the extent of actually being fixed and a rate manipulated flexibly have more in common with each other than either has with a free rate. The worry about "competitive exchange depreciation," properly understood, is an argument against managed flexibility, not against truly free rates. So is the curious worry (expressed, for example, by Otmar

Emminger, a member of the Board of Governors of the German Bundesbank) that under a generalized system of fluctuating rates, there would be no currency in which central banks could safely hold working balances for carrying out their stabilizing interventions in the market. A final worry due to glossing over the distinction between managed and free flexibility suggests that the whole problem of international liquidity might be worse under flexible exchange rates than under the present system of adjustable pegs. As Sir Roy Harrod has suggested, national authorities might actually need larger external reserves to cope with speculative capital movements incited by the uncertainties of the new system itself.

The criticisms just reviewed raise the question whether the system of managed flexibility might not combine the worst rather than the best features of the gold standard and of free exchange rates. It surely would lack the automaticity and impersonality of the otherwise quite different adjustment mechanisms of those two polar systems. This is one reason why it may be tactically unwise to advocate managed flexibility as a way of trying out genuine flexibility little by little and of approaching genuinely free exchange rates gradually as businessmen and central bankers become accustomed to the idea. That approach may boomerang because any unsatisfactory experience with managed flexibility is apt to be blamed on flexibility as such. This misinterpretation has occurred all too often: "the lessons of history" are commonly said to have discredited free exchange rates, although it was *managed* flexibility instead that prevailed in the episodes typically cited.

THE "BAND" PROPOSAL

Most of these same criticisms have also been applied to still another compromise, the proposal to let exchange rates fluctuate freely within a band of perhaps 5 percent or more on either side of parity. Again, the possible poor performance due to falling between two stools would be open to misinterpretation.

One of the chief arguments for the band system is that it would lessen the problem of one-way-option speculation. At present, with exchange rates held within less than 1 percent of parity, speculators can count on winning if an expected change in parity does take place and on breaking almost even if it does not. But with a wide band, speculators would realize that the rate could rebound substantially from whichever edge of the band it was pressing against. Speculation could prove costly if wrong.

Speculation might even be stabilizing. Given firm confidence that the band would hold, an exchange rate approaching one edge would seem more likely to rebound than to break through. Speculators would help cause the expected rebound—or might even keep the rate from nearing the edge of the band in the first place. Stabilizing speculation would reduce the need for official intervention and official reserves. So would nonspeculative exchange-rate variations within the band, since they should help adjust balances of payments and national economic structures to changed conditions. The band system would thus ease the problem of international liquidity.

It is far from certain, on the other hand, that speculation would be stabilizing. Situations could develop, for example, in which a stand-off between bullishness and bearishness on the home currency depended on confidence in successful defense of the lower edge of the band. Confidence might weaken, upsetting the standoff, because that defense was draining official reserves. With the exchange rate clinging to the lower edge, the very width of the band might emphasize the wrongness of the mid-band parity. The disadvantages of rigid pegging, including the danger of speculation on what had become almost a one-way option, would then appear. (But if free-market supply and demand were to keep the rate comfortably within the limits of the band, then those limits would be unnecessary.) Expectations concerning policy and market conditions have more material to feed on and to change sharply about under the band system, as under other compromise systems, than under a "hands-off" exchange-rate policy.

Another argument for the band scheme envisages greater scope for official forward-exchange-rate policy. The idea is that official support of the forward value of the home currency could prevent or reverse an outflow of funds by way of interest arbitrage that would otherwise exert downward pressure on the spot exchange rate and on the official gold and foreign-exchange reserves when home interest rates were lower than foreign rates or when bearish speculation against the home currency was active in the forward-exchange market. But as explained above, a forward rate cannot go outside the support limits of the spot rate if those limits command confidence, as they would if the policies pursued were successful. A widened range of spot fluctuation would permit a substantial forward premium on the home currency when it was wanted to retain or attract arbitrage funds.

An appraisal of this argument would require going even more deeply into technicalities than a full exposition of the argument itself. Suffice to say that the band does not appear to have a clear and important advantage of the kind claimed, after all, over the existing system of fairly narrow support limits. Nevertheless, the argument is interesting because it sees one particular inconvenience in tight spot-rate pegging and therefore recommends going part way toward free exchange rates.

Some other arguments for the band proposal also partially recognize the case for flexibility: the band system would supposedly hold down the size of the reserve gains and losses that sometimes advertise disequilibrium under narrowly pegged rates, and exchange-rate movements within a broadened band would indicate the growing strength or weakness of a currency and thus serve as one useful guideline for domestic financial policy. This last point is sometimes developed into the claim that the need to hold the exchange rate within the band exerts some anti-inflationary discipline. This argument is subject to much the same reservations here as when it is used in favor of the adjustable peg.

THE "CRAWLING PEG" AND OTHER COMPROMISES

The band scheme pure and simple could be combined with official smoothing operations: instead of leaving the rate free within the band, the authorities might intervene continuously to counter short-run random or speculative wobbles. A third element, the adjustable peg, might be added to the combination, yielding a scheme of managed flexibility within an adjustable band.

A more distinctive proposal envisages a crawling peg. The exchange rate would be pegged within narrow limits, as under the Bretton Woods system, but the parity and the two limits flanking it could be changed, either deliberately or by formula, perhaps as often as every day. Each day's parity might be a moving average of the actual daily exchange rates over a specified number of immediately preceding months. If changed conditions had made a currency definitely overvalued, its consequent bumping along the lower edge of its narrow band would pull down both the moving average and the band itself; in this way the rate could gradually approach a new equilibrium level. Details of the scheme would presumably be such as to hold the maximum change of an exchange rate under pressure to within a few percent a year. Exchange-rate variation could contribute to equilibrating the balance of payments in an orderly way, without speculation being incited by susceptibility of the rate to sudden sharp adjustments. Less happily, some incentives would also be created akin to those of deductions from or additions to interest rates in countries whose currencies were weakening or strengthening. If bothersome capital movements were not to result, actual interest rates would have to be kept higher in a weak-currency country and lower in a strong-currency country than they otherwise would be. This additional complication for domestic monetary-fiscal policy might prove a serious disadvantage of the crawling peg, especially when policy has a hard enough job merely straddling among full employment, growth, price-level stability, and other domestic goals. And in still requiring official intervention, the scheme would not solve—at best it would ease—the problem of international liquidity.

Many more variants of reform schemes have been proposed than can be surveyed here. Readers may find it an instructive exercise to devise additional schemes themselves, putting together new combinations of the features of schemes already described, and then to appraise the probable advantages and disadvantages of each.

POLITICAL ACCEPTABILITY

So far we have ignored one all-too-familiar line of appraisal—the supposed political feasibility, or acceptability to policy-makers and voters, of different proposals. For at least two reasons, "political impossibility" should not rule a proposal out of consideration. First, discussing how a proposed change is likely to work can be a useful pedagogical device. It can be a way of conveying and testing understanding of economic principles and the facts and logic they rest on. Secondly, "political impossibility" is not an inherent operating property of an economic arrangement. It may be overcome. If a particular arrangement really does have a more attractive set of operating properties than its rivals, experts and even policy-makers and voters may eventually come to understand that fact. If an economist, concerned with his own reputation for practicality and reasonableness, makes amateur assessments of political feasibility and accordingly recommends policies other than those he truly considers best, he is shirking the responsibilities of the expert he claims to be.

REFERENCES

1. AMERICAN ENTERPRISE INSTITUTE FOR PUBLIC POLICY RESEARCH. *International Payments Problems.* Washington, D. C.: 1966. This symposium contains papers and discussions by several economists.

2. NATIONAL INDUSTRIAL CONFERENCE BOARD CONVOCATION (October 1965). *Gold and World Monetary Problems.* New York: Macmillan, 1966. (See pages 127–128 for the cited observations of Otmar Emminger.)

3. ROY HARROD. *Reforming the World's Money.* New York: St. Martin's Press, 1965. Chapter 2.

4. GEORGE N. HALM. *The "Band" Proposal: The Limits of Permissible Exchange Rate Variations.* International Finance Section, Princeton University, 1965.

5. WILLIAM FELLNER. "On Limited Exchange-rate Flexibility." In Fellner and others, *Maintaining and Restoring Balance in International Payments.* Princeton University Press, 1966, pp. 111–122.

6. JOHN H. WILLIAMSON. *The Crawling Peg.* Essay No. 50; International Finance Section, Princeton University, 1965.

7. J. CARTER MURPHY. "Moderated Exchange Rate Variability." *National Banking Review,* III, December 1965, pp. 151–161.

8. LELAND B. YEAGER. "A Skeptical View of the 'Band' Proposal." *National Banking Review,* IV, March 1967, pp. 291–297.

9. HENRY N. GOLDSTEIN. "A Further Comment on an Aspect of the 'Band' Proposal." *National Banking Review,* IV, June 1967, pp. 511–513.

INDEX

Absolute efficiency, concept of, 2–3
Absorption approach, 55–57, 60, 63–64
Active money supply, 59
Adjustable-peg system, 138–141, 144, 147
African Development Bank, 104
Agency for International Development, 104
Appreciation, 14, 50, 52, 54, 61, 66, 92, 129
Arbitrage, 11–12, 15, 55, 76, 78
gold, 15, 58–60, 75–76
interest, 83–87, 103, 130, 146
and market breadth, 87–88
multilateral currency, 11
Asian Development Bank, 104

Balance of payments, 19–26
adjustable-peg system and, 140
adjustment processes, 44–71
absorption approach, 55–57, 60, 63–64
automatic, 44–45, 48, 49, 53, 61, 62, 66, 71
deflationary, 65, 71, 126
destruction of, 61–64
domestic financing and, 65–66
exchange-rate, 49–71, 124–135
gold standard and, 47–51, 59, 61–63, 65, 66, 71, 122–124, 138
income and, 45–47, 49, 51, 55, 58, 124
price levels and, 45–47, 49–52, 54, 55, 58, 124
credits and debits, 20–22
deficits and surpluses, 24–26
family, 23–24, 43–44
Liquidity concept, 28–33, 35, 36, 39
national, 43–44
Official Reserve Transactions concept, 31–36, 39
transactions, aspects of, 22–24
United States, 27–42, 93, 95, 96, 116
Balance-of-payments equilibrium, 24, 26, 54, 59, 79, 80, 122, 126, 129
Balassa, Bela, 79
Band proposal, 145–147
Bank deposits, 10, 16, 21–23, 28, 44, 45, 48, 65, 66, 71, 90, 108, 125
Bank of England, 92
Bank for International Settlements, 102
Basel Agreements, 102
Basic balance, concept of, 33
Basic deficit, concept of, 33
Bernstein Committee, 31–33
Bretton Woods Conference, 99, 103
Bretton Woods system, 138–141, 144, 147

Canadian Exchange Fund Account, 144
Capital exports, 21–23
Capital formation, 30
Capital imports, 21–23, 39
Capital movements, 21, 28–31, 33, 35–40, 47, 49
and anti-inflationary monetary policy, 129
free exchange rates and, 130
interest-sensitive, 128–129
restrictions on, 85, 129
voluntary, 38–39, 95, 109, 137
and trade adjustment, 57–61
Central banks, 11, 13, 14, 29–32, 56, 63–69, 71, 91–94, 96, 102, 109–110, 142, 145
Commercial banks, 31, 32, 64–67, 69–71, 125
Commodity exports and imports, 5, 20, 23, 37, 76
Commodity points, 76
Common Market, 104
Comparative advantage, principle of, 3–4, 6, 58, 59, 61
Compensating balances, principle of, 24
Competition, exchange rates and, 4–7, 11, 50, 53, 54
imperfections in, 6
and opportunity costs, 1–4, 6
and prices, 4–6, 54–55
Competitive exchange depreciation, 143, 144
Composite reserve unit, 117
Convertibility (*see* Currency convertibility)
Covered interest arbitrage, 83–87, 103, 130, 146
Crawling peg, 147–148
Credit rationing by banks, 85
Credit tranches, 100
Culbertson, J. M., 94
Currency convertibility, 15, 35–36, 62, 104
nonresident (external), 15–16, 104
two-way, 16, 91, 98

Defense spending, overseas, 25, 35–37, 39
Deflation, 49, 51, 52, 62, 71, 116–117, 124, 126
Depreciation, 13, 14, 50, 52–55, 60–61, 87, 88, 129, 132
competitive exchange, 143, 144
free-market, 54
Depressions, 50, 52, 62, 126, 127, 129, 130
Devaluation, 13–14, 29, 35, 39, 41, 53, 55, 56, 62, 86, 95, 105, 116–117, 130, 139–141